Financial Sobriety

REBUILDING YOUR RELATIONSHIP WITH MONEY
ONE STEP AT A TIME

Matthew David Grishman

Copyright © 2018 by Matthew David Grishman.

All rights reserved. No part of this publication may be reproduced, distributed or transmitted in any form or by any means, including photocopying, recording or other electronic or mechanical methods, without the prior written permission of the publisher, except in the case of brief quotations embodied in critical reviews and certain other noncommercial uses permitted by copyright law. For permission requests, write to the publisher at the address below. These materials are provided to you by Matthew David Grishman for informational purposes only and Matthew David Grishman expressly disclaims any and all liability arising out of or relating to your use of same. The provision of these materials does not constitute legal or investment advice and does not establish an attorney-client relationship between you and Matthew David Grishman. No tax advice is contained in these materials. You are solely responsible for ensuring the accuracy and completeness of all materials as well as the compliance, validity and enforceability of all materials under any applicable law. The advice and strategies found within may not be suitable for every situation. You are expressly advised to consult with a qualified attorney or other professional in making any such determination and to determine your legal or financial needs. No warranty of any kind, implied, expressed or statutory, including but not limited to the warranties of title and non-infringement of third-party rights, is given with respect to this publication.

Matthew David Grishman

www.gebhardtgroupinc.com

Financial Sobriety/Matthew David Grishman. —1st edition

ISBN 9781710555196

Gebhardt Group, Inc. is an independently owned and operated wealth management firm helping individuals and families navigate major life transitions. Our financial planning process, the investment strategies we recommend, and the insurance solutions we use are all custom fit to meet the needs of each individual client.

Advisory services offered through Gebhardt Group, Inc., a Registered Investment Adviser.

Investing involves risk, including the potential loss of principal. No investment strategy can guarantee a profit or protect against loss in periods of declining values. None of the information contained in this book shall constitute an offer to sell or solicit any offer to buy a security or any insurance product.

Any references to protection benefits or steady and reliable income streams refer only to fixed insurance products. They do not refer, in any way, to securities or investment advisory products. Life insurance and annuity guarantees are backed by the financial strength and claims-paying ability of the issuing insurance company. They are insurance products that may be subject to fees, surrender charges and holding periods which vary by insurance company. Life Insurance and annuities are not FDIC insured.

The information and opinions contained in this book are provided for informational purposes only and are not a solicitation to buy or sell any of the products mentioned. The information is not intended to be used as the sole basis for financial decisions, nor should it be construed as advice designed to meet the particular needs of an individual's situation. We do not offer tax, legal or estate planning services or advice.

CONTENTS

Introduction I
    Part I: The Rise and Fall of a Rockstar— A Journey of Self-Discovery v
    Part II: My Relationship with Myself and with Others Is Reborn— Anecdotes About Life, Human Connection, and Defining True Wealth vi
    Part III: My Relationship with Money— Building and Protecting Financial Wealth vi

PART I: THE RISE AND FALL OF A ROCKSTAR IX

    Putting on the Mask 1
    Take It Off! 5
    The Road to Authenticity and a New Meaning for Wealth 11
    The Making of the Mask 13

PART II: MY RELATIONSHIP WITH MYSELF AND WITH OTHERS IS REBORN 19

    The Epicenter of Feeling Wealthy 21
        Ask. Listen. Feel. 25
        Where has all the empathy gone? 28
        Maintaining Trust Over a Lifetime 29
        Principle #1: Show up early and prepared 30
        Principle #2: Do what you say 30
        Principle #3: Finish what you start 30
        Principle #4: Say please, thank you, and you're welcome 31
        Principle #5: When you make mistakes, own them and fix them 31
    The Interfering Ego 33
        Tommy Boy, my wingman 36
        Vinny, my victim 39
        Captain Corporate, my CEO 45
        Matty, my peacekeeper 46
        Saul, my skeptic 46

Separating from My Actors to Find the Epicenter of Connection 47
Quieting the Noise of Ego with a Power Source I Don't Understand 48
CAT'S IN THE CRADLE 53
WHAT I LEARNED FROM PA 57
The Core Values of True Wealth 59
TEACH YOUR CHILDREN 61
The Potential for Parents as Teachers 63
REALISTIC EXPECTATIONS VS. UNREALISTIC DEMANDS 69
Tip #1: Determine the Control Factor 70
Tip #2: Take the History Test 70
Tip #3: Stop Staring at the Horizon— Measure your Progress in Arears 71
SAY NO MORE 73
Say "No," More 74

PART III: MY RELATIONSHIP WITH MONEY 79

GETTING STARTED ON THE RIGHT PATH 81
Tip #1: Pay yourself first 81
Tip #2: Create your rainy-day fund 82
Tip #3: Buy health insurance 82
Tip #4: Contribute to a company-sponsored retirement plan or a Roth IRA 83
Tip #5: Treat your personal balance sheet like a business 86
Tip #6: Protect your credit 87
Tip #7: Spend meaningfully 88
Tip #8: Accept that you do not know everything 88
MIDDLE SCHOOL MATH FINALLY PAYS OFF 91
Stocks. Bonds. Mutual Funds. Exchange-Traded Funds. Annuities. Life Insurance 94
INVESTING IN STOCK 97
What is stock? 98
How do I purchase shares of stock? 99
How do I identify good stocks to buy? 100
Basic rules for stock owners 101
MAKING SENSE OF BONDS 103
Credit Risk 104

- Interest-Rate Risk 104
- Call Risk 105
- Reinvestment Risk and Inflation Risk 105
- MUTUAL FUNDS VS. EXCHANGE-TRADED FUNDS (ETFs) 111
  - Actively-Managed Mutual Funds 111
  - Passively-Managed Index Mutual Funds 113
  - What is an ETF? 114
  - ETFs Version 2.0 115
- IS AN ANNUITY RIGHT FOR ME? 117
- TO INSURE OR NOT TO INSURE 121
  - This Ain't Your Granddad's Life Insurance Anymore 126
- THIRTY-YEAR PLAN FOR A RETIREMENT ON PURPOSE 127
  - Financial Preparedness 128
  - Choice and Control 129
  - Purpose 131
- THE MULTI-PHASE RETIREMENT 135
  - The Go-Go Phase 137
  - The Slow-Go Phase 139
  - The No-Go Phase 139
- SUGGESTIONS FOR WOMEN IN TRANSITION—APPLIES TO MEN, TOO! 143
  - Tip #1: Give yourself time. 145
  - Tip #2: Ask for help. 145
  - Tip #3: Buy yourself financial safety. 146
  - Tip #4: Try to stay healthy. 146
  - Tip #5: Protect yourself. 146
- A THREAT TO FUTURE FINANCIAL SECURITY 149
- COMMON MYTHS THAT HURT RETIREMENT SAVERS 155
  - Myth #1: You must beat the market. 156
  - Myth #2: "Buy and hold" investing is the best approach. 157
  - Myth #3: Your broker has your back. 159
- CHALLENGING THE STATUS QUO 163
- BRINGING IT ALL TOGETHER 167
  - Xerox and Kodak 169

SOME FINAL THOUGHTS 173

ABOUT THE AUTHOR 175

This book is dedicated to the incredible people who touched my life in a very meaningful way and opened my heart to the meaning of true wealth. Amie, Miles and Lucas. Jill, Hank, Daniel, and Gillian. Jim, Beth, Emily, Grace, Jack, and Grant. Allison, Terrie, and Nancy. Vinnie, Spencer, Russell, Randy, Gary, and Bryan. Alan and Carol. Glen, Kurt, Phil, Brian, Chris, and Duane. Tricia, Paul, Elinor, Maura, Joe, Maggie, Michael, and Judy. Bo and Dawn. Jim Kelly.

Someone who deserves special recognition for my love of writing is my mother, Jill Grishman. Without her fostering in me a love for writing, this book would never have come to be. It is through her guidance and inspiration that I have been able to communicate through the written word. My mom was always there for me, peeking over my shoulder to help me interpret the world through writing. She encouraged me to always see things from various vantage points, how others may view things differently from me, and to write about those differences with honor and grace. My mom also taught me the basics of good grammar, spelling, punctuation, and sentence structure. She showed me how painting a vivid picture of words from the heart could be seen by others as an honest reflection of my innermost self. She taught me how to be vulnerable. My mom was always my advocate, my cheerleader, and my accountability. She was the Spartan Warrior mother I needed. I am eternally grateful.

~Matthew Grishman, Author

Introduction
ALL I EVER WANTED

All I ever wanted was three things:
- to be liked
- to be recognized
- to be rich

My first real job earning a regular paycheck was as a dishwasher at Dick's Subs in Schenectady, New York. I was sixteen years old. That first paycheck in my hands was a rush of instant satisfaction. It felt so good. Much like an alcoholic obsesses over the next drink, my next paycheck couldn't come soon enough. Money got its hooks into me the instant I had some—and having *some* was never enough.

I did a lot of rationalizing in my early days of chasing money. I had a storyline to justify my constant craving for more money, one that stuck for years. I was absolutely convinced: If I made tons of money, I could take care of the people in my life and shroud them with comfort and ease. If I could do that for my people (and be recognized for it as their hero), then I'd be able to look in the mirror and feel proud of the dude staring back at me. This thought process worked for me for a long time.

As my income started booming in my late twenties and early thirties, the subtle effects of "lifestyle inflation" sneaked up behind me. At this point in my life, I was unaware of this form of inflation and the long-term damage it could cause to my relationships—both with money, and with those I was closest to. At the time, though, I had one singular focus. I didn't just want to keep up with the Joneses; I wanted to *be* Mr. Jones.

As I continued chasing this dream of being rich, loved, and recognized by everyone, I began to feel a disconnect between what I saw on the outside and what I felt on the inside. Rather than dealing with that lack of congruency in a healthy way, I drove the feelings away by acquiring more. When acquiring more wasn't enough, I began to drink and eat to numb the pain that was no longer satisfied by purchasing meaningless stuff.

My relentless pursuit of money, recognition, and love not only cost me nearly everything I had amassed financially, but it also damaged my most important personal relationships. Most critically, the one I had with myself. I reached a point where I hated the face staring back at me in the mirror. By 2005, an outside view may have shown that I was at the top of the mountain; I had arrived. But on the inside, I had reached a critical bottom with untreated spendaholic, foodaholic, and alcoholic behaviors.

Some people reach the bottom and wind up dead or locked in prison. I'm lucky to have reached the bottom well before either of those two points, but make no mistake: at one time, I was headed toward one or both. For me, bottom was being completely broke, lacking a single dollar of purchasing power, while having a wife and two young sons depending upon me. I had let them down. I had failed them. My self-centered behaviors wound up ripping through their lives like a tornado. It took all I could to seek help and begin to repair the damage I had caused to the people I loved most.

Fixing the damage I caused required me to completely surrender my old way of thinking. It required me to learn the true meaning of wealth. I had to learn how to forgive myself. I had to learn to place much greater value on my relationships and experiences than I did on the things in my possession. I had to learn to use a new muscle called discipline to make better choices, despite my impulsive desires to acquire more stuff. Not only did I stop acquiring meaningless stuff, I began giving away more of my personal possessions. Although mostly symbolic, giving away my stuff freed me to acquire deeper, more meaningful relationships and experiences. By saying no to things, it allowed me to say yes to people and experiences that truly enriched my life.

Among those enriching experiences were those I had with a man who offered me hope in my darkest hours. Through his empathy and compassion, I was able to learn what true wealth was about. So much so that now I get to stand shoulder-to-shoulder with that man, Jim Gebhardt, and help do for others what he did for me. Through our Wealth F.O.R.M.ation Experience™ at Gebhardt Group, Inc., we help people navigate some of their most challenging life transitions. My transition was from a lifestyle of self-centered thinking and hedonistic spending that left me almost bankrupt (morally *and* financially) to an abundantly wealthy life of investing in myself and others so I could have as much positive impact on the world as possible.

For the people I now serve, some experience a transition similar to mine. Others experience the death of a loved one, or the end of meaningful relationships through divorce or a failed business partnership. Some are overwhelmed with the prospects of retirement and are trying to figure out the day-to-day pieces of Life 2.0, answering questions like, "Have I saved enough money?" and, "What am I supposed to do with myself for the next thirty years, now that everything's changed?"

I wrote this book because there are people out there who were unexpectedly thrown into a major life transition, as was I. They may share a story similar to mine, or their life challenges and circumstances could be completely different. Regardless, many people I meet are living lives that look great on the outside but are filled with devastating internal pain. This pain affects all aspects of life, especially close personal relationships, satisfaction and success at work, and the ability to have real fun in life.

An unexpected transition can also create a misguided belief system about money. If my experience can help create a renewed sense of strength and hope for others, then I will have done my job by sharing my story.

My purpose in life—my reason for existence—is to challenge conventional thinking and inspire others to do the same. My transformed beliefs about our relationships with self, others, and money are counter to our current cultural norms. It wasn't easy to allow myself to be completely vulnerable to everyone and to reveal the internal angst I was experiencing, but it was required for me to make the changes I desired in my life.

Maybe, like me, you have spent years or possibly decades lying to yourself and others. Perhaps like me, your insides do not always match your outsides. Maybe the lack of personal congruency has led you to a life of overeating, alcohol abuse, and/or compulsive spending. The self-deception may run so deep you may even believe your "outside," or the part of yourself you show to the world, to be your real-life story. If this is you, I feel your inner turmoil. I feel your conflict—I know your shame.

But beside the anguish I carried with me in my self-deception, I also felt the subtle glow of a beautiful person who was hiding behind a mask, someone who wanted to give his gifts to the world; a person who was starving for authenticity and a simpler life of true wealth and genuine happiness.

By choosing to read this book, you've taken a huge first step. Despite the fear of the unknown that lies ahead, I hope you feel some degree of pride knowing you are developing an awareness and a curiosity of what life could be. But I get it—what lies ahead is a scary unknown. You might be wondering, *"What if the world finds out I'm not the person everyone thinks I am, that I'm not as rich, smart, strong, or successful as they all think I am? Will people turn their back on me? Will I wake up one day all alone?"*

I don't have a concrete answer for you. All I can share with you is my experience. There are certainly days now when I feel lonely in my experience; I have learned there are not many out there who have braved the path to finding true wealth. Sometimes the lonely path can really suck. But—and it's a big *BUT*—I am sober in every aspect of my life. I look in the mirror every day and love the imperfect man staring back at me. I am surrounded by an intimate circle of people who love and trust me. I experience joy and laughter every day of my life. I have a much healthier relationship with money and have learned to use it to accomplish amazing things and enjoy fulfilling experiences.

As I cleaned up the wreckage of my past and began to live authentically, many old doors closed, but others opened. Many people fell out of my life. Several new people appeared. Finding the path to true wealth and happiness invites those who are meant to be in your life and repels those who are not.

Be brave. Have faith. If you're reading this book, I'm guessing you want to change some or all aspects of how wealth is represented in your life. My primary goal in writing this book is to help people rebuild wealth by gaining complete clarity on the three main components, or relationships, that make up wealth; relationship with self, relationship with others, and relationship with money.

Here's what's to come in the chapters ahead:

PART I: THE RISE AND FALL OF A ROCKSTAR— A JOURNEY OF SELF-DISCOVERY

For me, the journey toward finding true wealth began with healing my innermost relationship with myself—I had to re-learn how to love and forgive the man in the mirror. Becoming aware of who I was and who I was not was a painstaking, eye-opening experience.

I'll share with you my personal story that led me down the path of superstardom (in my own mind, of course) followed by the destructive behaviors that nearly destroyed those three most important relationships I have: my relationship with me, my relationship with others, my relationship with money.

PART II: MY RELATIONSHIP WITH MYSELF AND WITH OTHERS IS REBORN—ANECDOTES ABOUT LIFE, HUMAN CONNECTION, AND DEFINING TRUE WEALTH

Part II dives into the great transformation of how learning to love myself influenced my ability to love others. I'll share specifics about my relationships with some key people in my life and how I began to repair those relationships that were damaged by my destructive behaviors. You'll discover the beliefs I've developed about living a wealthy life based on real experiences and genuine human connection.

Everyone needs to learn the hard way, sometimes by experiencing the consequences of a bad choice. But if my personal adventures can help one person avoid making a bad choice in their relationships with other people, then becoming vulnerable and writing this part of the book was well worth it.

PART III: MY RELATIONSHIP WITH MONEY— BUILDING AND PROTECTING FINANCIAL WEALTH

This section of the book is about how to build the financial security component of true wealth. This is the part of the book where I share the how-to's for exactly how I was able to rebuild my financial security. Despite my being a financial mess at times, two decades in the financial industry have taught me how to save and invest successfully. I haven't always followed my own advice, but what I share here are simple wealth building strategies that are designed to be successful.

Many of us are asking ourselves questions like:
- How do I even begin to rebuild my wealth?
- How do I begin building it for the first time?
- What mistakes am I okay making along the way?
- What mistakes do I need to avoid at all costs?
- I have plenty of income, but where the heck has it gone by the end of each month?

Part III will help you discover answers to these very questions. Even if you find yourself still unsure after reading this section, you will at least have the foundation of knowledge to know where to look for answers to your remaining questions. Not every chapter is meant for every reader. Some chapters will be relevant to you now, and others may be more relevant down the road or for someone else you know.

Are you ready to seek a whole new world of wealth and abundance? If you're willing to open your mind and your heart to a new way of living when it comes to wealth, then now is *your* time to define what wealth looks like for you.

Part I

The Rise and Fall of a Rockstar
A JOURNEY OF SELF-DISCOVERY

Putting on the Mask

It was 1995 and all I dreamed about was being filthy rich. At that time, Gordon Gecko, the fictional villain from the 80s movie *Wall Street*, was my hero. The potential fame and fortune of working as a stockbroker on Wall Street sucked me in just after graduating college.

I remember my first boss, Jon N., telling me, "Listen here, Rookie. You wanna make it in this business?"

"Of course, Mr. N," I responded.

"Then get your ass married as soon as possible. Pump out a few kids and buy a big house you can't afford. Get yourself a hot set of wheels you can't afford, either. That's my guarantee you'll show up to work every day and dial your ass off."

As the first new trainee in my firm's Darien, Connecticut, office in several years, I was surrounded by superstar veteran brokers: fast-talking, stock-pitching, IPO-slinging hot shots. Everyone in my office drove a Mercedes Benz S class or a BMW 7 Series. Most kept a collection of monogrammed French cuff shirts hanging in the closet of their office. Mr. N's advice seemed logical; live like the rock star you want to be. But since I struggled with believing in myself, I wasn't convinced I was cut out for being a broker. I took my time with Jon's "shopping list" for starving young rookies.

Although my self-doubt was something that would hold me back for many more years, that delay in overextending myself paid off at the time. After dialing numbers into my phone over 300 times a day for an entire year, I was ready to call it quits as a broker. I was so bad at it that eventually I absolutely detested cold calling. No matter how much allure the lifestyle on display around me had, I couldn't find the courage to pick up the phone and hear one more person say, "NO—Fuck off!"

Facing such a disastrous defeat, I asked myself how I was ever going to realize my dream of living like a rock star. I hadn't dialed the phone in weeks. I knew I was days away from losing my job for lack of dials. I had no idea what would be next for me.

Then *next* showed up.

Paul S. walked into my office on a Tuesday morning. Paul was a young sales rep—or, in his words, a "Mutual Fund Wholesaler," for an up-and-coming mutual fund firm based in New York City. His job was to sell us on the merits of placing my clients' investment assets in his firm's care by purchasing shares of their mutual fund lineup. I had seen lots of these wholesaler types come in and out of my office over the months prior. They were generally old, stuffy Wall Street guys who paid little attention to rookies like me but fell all over the corner-office brokers, taking them out for three-martini lunches, backslapping, swapping stories, and comparing country club days and misadventures across the globe.

Paul was different. Paul was twenty-seven years old and delivered a presentation to the brokers in my office that had me hanging on every word. Since at the time I knew little about mutual funds, I didn't actually understand what he was talking about. But man, did he sound smooth. And he looked like a million bucks. While other wholesalers were crusty and stale, Paul wore a sharp pinstripe suit with a crisp white button down and the shiniest wing-tip shoes I had ever seen. He wasn't overstated like the guys in my office either, with their French cuffs and absurdly loud ties. Rather, he looked like a real pro from Wall Street: not overdressed, simply understated and striking. And he paid attention to *me*!

After the presentation, I asked Paul to visit with me in my office.

"Paul, tell me how you got into wholesaling for a mutual fund company?" I asked.

"Simple," he said. "I saw an ad in the New York Times about internal sales jobs. I interviewed. I got hired. Two years later, I relocated to Boston and got my own outside sales territory to run."

Paul spent an hour and a half answering my questions about his life as a mutual fund wholesaler. It sounded too good to be true. Paul lived in the Back Bay of Boston in an upscale condo. He made just over a quarter of a million dollars a year traveling around the Northeast meeting with brokers like me every day. His firm gave him amazing benefits and a six-figure travel-and-entertainment budget. He was new to the career. Paul hypnotized me with his visions of making millions by earning himself a seat at the partners' table of his mutual fund firm by the age of thirty-five.

The more Paul spoke, the more I knew this was the path for me. I was done living on my $400-a-week draw and eating ramen noodles for dinner every night. I was done dialing a telephone hundreds of times a day to beg strangers for their business. It was time for me to accelerate my progress toward living my dream.

"Guess what, Matt?" Paul said enticingly, as if reading my mind, "We're hiring."

Paul told me his company needed trainees to work in their Manhattan office and, one day, move out into their own territory somewhere in the U.S., doing exactly what Paul was doing.

"Are you for real?" I was skeptical about being worthy of his offer.

"I am. And you're exactly the person we're looking for." He saw something in me I could not. "May I introduce you to my boss?"

With curiosity and a little hope poking through my lack of self-esteem, I stumbled over my words. "Uh, um, yeah . . . I mean, yes, of course you can."

Paul smiled and whipped out his very cool (at the time) Motorola flip phone. He called his manager right there in my office to facilitate an introduction. Things moved quickly. That afternoon I bought myself a navy pinstripe suit, polished my resume and wingtips, and prepared for the moment when I would head off to New York to explore my new career options as a wholesaler in the financial services industry. That moment came the following Monday.

Fast forward seventeen years, and life as a wholesaler was everything I had imagined it would be. I had climbed the ladder through a few firms and had reached the pinnacle of investment wholesaling. I had earned the title of Senior Vice President and was tapped on the shoulder to be a national spokesperson for one of the largest insurance companies in the world. I was paid the big bucks. My high six-figure income let me wear $2,000 suits and a fancy collection of Rolex watches. I drove sexy European cars and flew first class. I was pampered with outstanding meals and slugged $300 bottles of wine like they were grape juice. I got married to the most beautiful woman in the world, built her a giant house, and had a couple of kids who wore designer clothing from birth. My wife, Amie, spent without the burden of a monthly budget. This was starting to look exactly like the picture my first manager, Jon, had painted for me.

I had arrived—I was living my dream.

Take It Off!

I got to the top by learning how to tell a relatable story, by inspiring enthusiasm in everyone I met, and by strutting down the street like I was a king. I had everything I ever wanted: money, power, influence, and respect. I was finally living the life of an absolute rock star—the real American dream—at the top of Wall Street's financial food chain.

Or so I thought.

It was July 2005 and I was standing in my bathroom, admiring myself in the mirror. I was waiting for a limo to pick me up. I was two hours away from boarding a flight to Southern California, where I was scheduled to speak in front a large audience of financial advisors at an industry conference that would occupy the entire San Diego Convention Center.

A few minutes before I was scheduled for pickup, my wife Amie reminded me to stop at the bank on my way to the airport to get out some cash, since I had forgotten to do so the day before.

I quickly scanned my bank account balance on my laptop to see which account I would pull the money from. I knew I had been charging up a storm and throwing cash around like it grew on a tree in my back yard, but up until then, I had been unaware of the exact amount I had spent.

Holy shit!

My savings account was empty.

My checking account was overdrawn by $210.

That had to be a mistake. There was no way that could have happened. It must have been a mistake on the bank's part. Amie would have to handle that and get it fixed, since I was on my way out of town. The solution for now was simple: a cash advance from one of my three credit cards.

Holy shit again!

Chase Visa, credit limit $20,000. Maxed out.

Wells Fargo Visa, credit limit $15,000. Maxed out.

Capital One Visa, credit limit $10,000. Maxed out.

I was shocked and completely frozen. Time had come to a screeching halt. A few minutes felt like an hour. As my heart began to race, pushing all the blood in my body to my head, the realization hit me that the bank error was not an error. I was actually overdrawn on my bank accounts *and* I was maxed out on my credit cards with no paycheck in sight for *three more weeks*. Panic.

Thoughts began racing inside my head. I had zero purchasing power. How was I supposed to fly to San Diego and represent a Fortune 100 company in front of a room full of financial advisors? I thought my heart was going to explode out of my chest. Sweat was now pouring down my face onto my handmade silk tie. My vision began to blur from the edges of my periphery until all I could see was a narrow tunnel of dim light. Was that the light at the end of the tunnel I've always heard about, or was it a train headed my way?

My knees eventually gave out and I fell to the floor. I was convinced I was having a heart attack.

I lay on the floor in my Hickey Freeman suit, coming to terms with the fact that I was going to die right here, right now on my bathroom floor. As the panic completely overwhelmed me, I called out for Amie. I found the few words needed to tell her what was happening.

"How the hell am I going to check into my hotel tonight? How am I going to pay for a cab from the airport to my hotel? How am I going to eat?"

Amie didn't have an answer. She just began to cry.

A few more minutes passed that felt like hours. Once I realized I wasn't dying from a major heart attack, I pulled my phone out of my pocket and called my boss.

"John, I can't make it to San Diego."

"What?" he shouted. I pulled the phone away from my ear.

In my shaky voice, I muttered, "I'm sick as a dog. I woke up with a bad stomach bug and I can't leave my bathroom, let alone board a plane. I think I have the flu."

"Oh man, that's horrible timing," John said. He was a twenty-five-year company loyalist, and the company always came first.

"Okay. Feel better, I guess, and take care of yourself. We'll find another speaker."

At the time, I felt I had no choice but to lie. He bought it. Temporary relief was mine. But as I hung up the phone, it dawned on me that my entire life as a Wall Street Rockstar was one big fairy tale.

The shame began to build right away. The combined reality of being broke and completely full of shit for most of my life started to sink in. I led everyone to believe I had the world at my feet. Yet there I was, a useless puddle of failure, curled up on my bathroom floor in my $2,000 suit, wishing I were dead.

I didn't know what to do next. I did not have the purchasing power to buy groceries or pay a $10 copay at the pediatrician if my kids got sick, even if I could have gassed up my car to go anywhere in the first place. I already owed my parents close to $50,000 for bailing me out of a mortgage mess in 2002, so there was no way I was going to call them for more help. I had way too much pride to call any of my colleagues or friends. I had been making a high six-figure income for more than a decade, helping financial advisors make better investment decisions for their clients, and I was broke.

Maybe I was just flat-out broken.

With a half tank of gas left in my car, I decided to go for a drive and think. I had to figure something out. I drove recklessly, overwhelmed with irrational thoughts. I couldn't come up with any logical answers. I blew through red lights and stop signs, speeding, cutting off other drivers, oblivious to the world around me. It was a miracle I didn't kill anyone. My brain spun in circles and I glared at myself in the rear-view mirror with complete disdain.

"You are such a loser. You are a complete failure!" I said to myself over and over.

I felt like the worst human being on the planet. I wondered if I should veer into oncoming traffic or drive off a high embankment. Amie and the kids would collect $4 million in life insurance and everything would be okay for them, financially. The pain and disgust would go away for me, too. But every time I considered steering my car into oncoming traffic, I couldn't do it. I was such a low-life loser who had lost control over everything. My life had become so unmanageable that I couldn't even kill myself when I wanted to.

I felt completely hopeless.

With my gas tank now running low, I gave up my quest for solutions and headed home to beg my wife's forgiveness. I walked in the front door and it was obvious she was scared and angry. Amie, the most beautiful creature in existence, tears puddling under her eyes, sat clutching our two boys while they cried in her arms. Miles, who was five at the time, gripped his favorite stuffed puppy, and Lucas, my little Lukie Dukie, was wedged between them in his Toy Story pajamas.

"Where were you, Daddy?" Miles asked.

Before I could mutter an answer, Amie shouted, "I can't believe it. We're out of money? Are you kidding me?"

"I'm so sorry, honey. I'm so sorry. I'll fix this. I promise."

The yelling and crying continued for a while, until exhaustion took over and we declared a temporary truce. We turned our attention to calming our boys and helping them get to bed. I was surprised Amie didn't kick me out of the house. Instead, she decided we would hunker down at home for a few weeks with just our family of four. We were going to figure out how we got into this mess and how we were going to get out of it.

We didn't go out. We didn't see friends. We spent a lot of time over the next few weeks in silence. After some discussion, Amie and I came to an agreement about what we needed to do. I messed up. I had made millions of dollars and squandered most of it on meaningless stuff. It was important for me to own my mistakes and do whatever it took to fix them.

It was during this painful time that I first began to understand the true meaning of wealth.

I was finally at a point of desperation and, for a moment, my pride stepped aside. I called one of my closest friends, who happened to be a financial advisor, and I begged him for his help. He was the only one I could trust, and I was willing to do whatever he suggested.

"What's up? What do you need?" Jim asked when I called. I'm sure he hadn't anticipated the frank, humbling conversation that came after. Thankfully, Jim was willing and able to help us.

He started us on an "austerity diet." I was never good at dieting, but I was out of other options. No more frivolous spending. No more expensive dinners.

But as I was to learn, my spending was just a symptom of a much larger demon brewing inside me. Jim introduced me to his life coach, Jim Kelly. It was on our first call together that I heard the question that would change the entire direction of my life.

Jim Kelly asked me point blank, "Matthew, when are you going to stop lying and start telling the truth to yourself and the whole world?"

I was struck. It was as though he'd seen my deepest wound, and he didn't even know me. I said, "To hell with you!" and hung up the phone.

The truth hurt.

Yet despite my denial, I felt something inside me begin to shift. Within a few minutes of slamming the phone down on Jim, I called him back.

"I'm so sorry, Jim. I didn't mean to hang up on you like a complete jerk. Please tell me more about what you just said to me."

Jim responded gently, with a slight chuckle. "Take it off, Matthew."

"Take what off?" I asked.

Jim said, "The mask you've been wearing your whole life. Take it off and let the world see the beautiful, imperfect you that it's been waiting for."

As scary as that was even to consider, I realized at that moment that most of my life had been spent hiding from the truth. The way I dressed, the way I acted, the way I carried myself every day . . . it was one big facade that kept the real me hidden away from the world.

I wasn't exactly sure why I made the choice to hide behind my mask, but I knew it was finally time to take it off.

The Road to Authenticity and a New Meaning for Wealth

Two years had gone by since hitting my financial bottom, and by the end of 2007, I felt as if I had the foundation in place to turn my life around. I didn't hate myself like I used to. I was telling the truth. I had reached an all-new high point in my self-esteem after earning the most money I had ever earned in my career. It wasn't the big paycheck that made me stand taller, it was what I did with the paycheck that made me feel good.

My new money habits were firmly taking root. When it was time to replace my seven-year-old Audi, I purchased a gently used Ford Crown Victoria for $11,400. I got teased by some of my old colleagues and clients, but the choice to drive within my means was well worth the temporary torment I received from others.

I even remember one client saying to me, "Dude, are they not paying you anymore?"

I responded, "Yes, of course they're paying me. In fact, it's more money than I've ever earned. It's just I put my money in the bank rather than seeing it depreciate in a ridiculous car."

I learned throughout this entire ordeal that there are two kinds of pain in this world: the pain of discipline and the pain of regret. I also learned you can only avoid one of them. I made a choice that going forward I would choose more carefully. I had lived with the excruciating pain of regret for so many years.

Choosing the pain of discipline and allowing our advisor, Jim, to hold us accountable, Amie and I were able to completely reverse course and build the kind of true wealth we had always dreamed about. This was not an easy process. We lived frugally, often having little extra money to do anything beyond basic subsistence. We had debts to pay and savings to replenish. But in sticking to our plan, by 2011, I was able to walk away from corporate America and do what it was I was really put on this earth to do for others:

Be the best money and relationship advisor I am capable of becoming.

Today I have the privilege of helping people manage life's most challenging transitions, be it death of a loved one, divorce, relocation, retirement . . . any unexpected or unplanned circumstance that sends a family into limbo. A good day for me is any day I help someone heal or improve their relationships with their loved ones and their money.

By telling my stories and becoming completely vulnerable to the world, I healed from the wounds of my past and have since helped others take that first step in doing the same. When talking with others about their experiences, the same questions continue to come up in almost every conversation.

"Matt, what the heck happened in your life that led you down this path? Why did you feel the need to lie to the whole world and make up this rockstar image of who you thought the world wanted to know? When did you put your mask on?"

This is what I tell them.

The Making of the Mask

At ten years old, I was the target of two bullies on the playground of my elementary school. Their names were Gerry and Joe. Gerry was the little ring leader. Joe was his muscle man.

I was different from these boys. I was a Jewish kid from the city with affluent, educated parents, and here we were living in a small farming community in upstate New York. My dad was the superintendent of schools and one of the highest-paid people in town. As a public figure, his salary was published annually in the local newspaper for everyone to read.

Day after day, these two little tormenters terrorized me. Some days they threw anti-Semitic slurs in my face, other days it was their fists. Every day in fifth and sixth grade, they chased me around the playground while the other kids just watched and laughed.

"Where you running to, Jew Boy?" Gerry used to say. "Hey! Come here, Jew. I want to see if you have horns on your forehead like all the other Jews." To my knowledge, I was the only Jewish kid Gerry had ever met.

I was confused, and I was afraid. I thought that if I told my teacher, Joe and Gerry would surely kill me.

My dad tried to help, but his advice was frightening: "If someone hits you, hit them back." I knew I had no choice—eventually I would have to face them if I wanted to put an end to the bullying. The game of cat and mouse played out for a few years, but there was ultimately a day of reckoning.

In small towns, high school football games are the final word of community events. Attendance is just shy of mandatory for school officials, parents, students, the socially involved, and anyone who is anyone. My dad and I were standing on the 50-yard line of our high school field when Gerry and Joe approached.

Gerry had this stupid grin on his face. "Hey Jew boy," he whispered. "Wanna fight?"

"No, I do not," I responded.

"Well, we're going to kick your ass tonight anyway. Either fight back or lay there and take your beating. Doesn't matter to me."

I had enough. I looked over at my dad, who was unaware of the conversation and the heavy, cold sweat that had started to radiate across my body. I shook my head, shrugged my shoulders and let out a big sigh of air. I followed Gerry and Joe to the parking lot behind the football field. Something in me had snapped.

"You ready, Jew? You are dead meat," said Gerry.

As he lunged toward me, I cocked my arm back and hit him as hard as I could. Direct contact to the stomach. A loud, long breath came spewing out of his mouth as he dropped to his knees.

Joe froze and looked at me with eyes as big as dinner plates, his mouth hanging wide open in complete disbelief. My heart throbbed in my throat; adrenaline coursed through my body. I couldn't believe what I had just done.

As I stood there trembling, Joe scooped Gerry up off the ground, slung him over his shoulder and ran in the opposite direction. I could hear Joe's clomping feet and Gerry's gasps for air gradually fade as they disappeared into the woods behind the high school.

Was that it? Was that finally the end of three hostile years of bullying by Gerry and Joe? It was, and I decided I would never let this happen to me ever again. Rather than being myself and taking the risk that someone else might bully me for it, I decided to protect myself from future bullying by hiding the real me from the rest of the world. By age twelve, I chose to create a persona that hid the awful truth of who I was and blended me in with everyone else. In fact, behind my mask, I was going to go way beyond "normalcy" by being the coolest, smartest, bravest kid in my school, even if that meant making up stories and telling flat-out lies.

At the end of ninth grade, my dad got a new job far from the school where I had been bullied. There I met new kids and made instant friends. My mask-wearing strategy was working. On the outside, everyone at my new school admired me. They saw a fifteen-year-old "Renaissance man" who came from wealth and who was already a world-traveler. Granted, most of my stories were just that—stories, planned for peak coolness. I quickly became the center of the party, and all the popular kids wanted to hang out with me.

As I grew older, finished college, and began making some serious money, my life as a rock star reached a new level. Every weekend was spent partying like it was New Year's Eve, and I paid the bill. To keep my mask on and keep the party going, I threw money around and continued creating stories that wowed my growing circle of followers.

Despite all the comfort I had bought myself and all the fun I was having, I began to feel empty inside. My spending grew to epic proportions. Alcohol and drugs became my daily pain killers for the hurt I was feeling inside. The life of the mask-yielding rock star hit all new false heights. The entire world saw the epitome of success; all I saw was a lying worthless failure who needed alcohol and pills to feel good about himself enough to continue hiding in plain sight.

Until that disastrous day in 2005 when I hit my financial bottom, I showed the world who I wanted them to see. It was from the financial tragedy that almost destroyed my family that I took my first step forward. I started by telling myself the truth and took on the risk of letting the world see the real me: a far-from-perfect bullied kid who still makes mistakes every day and feels sadness and anger as often as he feels happiness and excitement.

Identifying that trigger moment in my life and choosing to move forward with courage, forgiveness, and gratitude (and a lot of help from the people I love most) is what brought me to tell my most personal stories. I have long since forgiven Gerry and Joe. I think about them both often and hope they found the love and respect in their lives that they were both so desperately and obviously craving. It was through forgiving them that I first realized nothing in life happens *to* me; everything happens *for* me. The bullying from Gerry and Joe happened *for* me. It helped me see every human expression at its core is either an expression *of love* or a cry out *for love*. As cruel and misguided as it may have felt at the time, the bullying by Gerry and Joe was nothing more than a desperate cry for love.

In 2005, I hit bottom and began my recovery as a spendaholic. I've relapsed many times. But today I feel proud of what I've accomplished. I am a wealthy man who lives in a modest house. I drive a not-so-brand-new Dodge pickup and arrive at work most days wearing blue jeans and sneakers. I have completely redefined what true wealth means to me. It's not just a measure of financial success anymore. It's about the four most important *personal values* in my life: family, occupation, recreation, and beliefs about money.

- My ***family*** is my foundation. It's rock solid and I am surrounded by people I love. The people in my life feed my soul and give me a deep sense of **human connection**.

- My ***occupation*** gives me a great sense of ***purpose*** as I make a difference in the lives of those I serve.

- ***Recreation*** is an everyday occurrence. I have *fun* doing the things I love with the people I love in my favorite places. Laughter is my daily prescription.

- I have developed new beliefs about ***money***. Money is a precious resource that gives me a sense of ***financial security***. I have learned how to save it and use it for the important things in life, like vacationing with my family, educating my kids, and building a business that employs and helps others in my community.

Am I perfect? Not even close. Even as an owner of a wealth management firm, I still make an occasional poor choice when it comes to money, but that's part of being human and a recovering spendaholic. It's about progress, not perfection. Relapse is a big part of my story and my continual growth. Thankfully, Amie believes in me and accepts me fully for who I am. My boys fill my heart with endless amounts of gratitude as they remind me every day of the simple gifts of love and laughter. My Mom, Jill; my Dad, Hank; and my brother, Daniel have always shown me unconditional love and encouragement, despite my old deceptive ways. Finally, I still have my dearest friend and financial advisor, Jim Gebhardt, in my life. Jim happens to be my business partner now, working by my side and inspiring me every day so I can do the work I was meant to do for others.

I will forever be grateful for Jim Kelly, the incredibly kind and patient coach who showed me the meaning of authenticity. Despite passing away a few years ago, his light shines genuinely through me every day.

Part II

My Relationship with Myself and with Others Is Reborn

ANECDOTES ABOUT LIFE, HUMAN CONNECTION, AND DEFINING TRUE WEALTH

The Epicenter of Feeling Wealthy

Over the course of my adult life, I have experienced the vastness of what it feels like to be at the top of the financial food chain, near the brink of personal bankruptcy, and almost everywhere in between. As I write this, I am somewhere along the upper bands of "in between" as it relates to my financial well-being. My business is flourishing. I have money in the bank. Thanks to my wife, Amie, and her full-time employment, we have excellent health insurance. My spending is less than I'm earning most months. I pay my bills on time. I am well on my way to being debt free.

I am financially secure.

I feel very wealthy.

This was not always the case. There were times in my life when I made more money in a year than many people make in a lifetime, yet at that time I did not feel wealthy. There were times I possessed things that were the envy of many others, yet at that time I did not feel wealthy. For so many years, I spent my time consumed with making money and buying stuff, trying to fill an unsatisfied void that continued to grow each and every day. Sure, the things I bought and the large paychecks I received left me feeling temporarily satisfied. But in a short period of time, my hunger would return and my need for more money and more stuff would be back in full force.

Have you ever felt a similar feeling?

For me it was like constantly, compulsively eating junk food. I love a good Big Mac. It's super tasty and satisfying, especially when I haven't eaten all day and all I can think about is chomping into a juicy burger. But within an hour of eating a Big Mac (or two or three), I'm hungry again. It took me a long time to realize that eating healthy protein and big servings of vegetables (sautéed in salt and butter, of course) was just as tasty as a Big Mac. But I didn't find myself starving again so quickly after eating them. Those healthier, more substantive meals left me satiated for extended periods of time.

Chasing money and buying stuff left me feeling much the same way as the Mac: temporarily satisfied and starving a short time later.

What was I missing that might help me stay financially satiated for longer periods of time without having to always chase money and things to feel full?

It's not my intention to argue that money is not an important part of wealth. It certainly can be a big part of feeling wealthy. The amount of money I have at my disposal and the amount of income I am creating for my family certainly has an impact on how wealthy I feel. But it's not the only source, nor the primary source, for why I am wealthy today.

As we continue to explore the concepts of Financial Sobriety and what it means to me to feel wealthy, I'm going to introduce the things that make up my true wealth and how I've been taught to account for them. If my experience connects with you, then I hope you can use my "accounting" methods as a template for yourself.

Money is the only aspect of my true wealth that can be measured in a traditional sense of dollars, percentages, and timeframes. But there are big contributors to my overall sense of *feeling* wealthy that cannot be measured this way. For me, they have been accounted for in alternative ways, mainly through feelings, observations, intuition, and feedback I receive from others I trust.

Money in the bank, mastery of my craft, knowledge about the world around me, wisdom, and a relentless work ethic all contribute to my sense of wealth. But for me the single greatest contributor to my wealth has come from **my connection with people and my desire to have real relationships**. If I were to estimate the breakdown of what comprises my true wealth from a traditionalist viewpoint, it would look something like this:

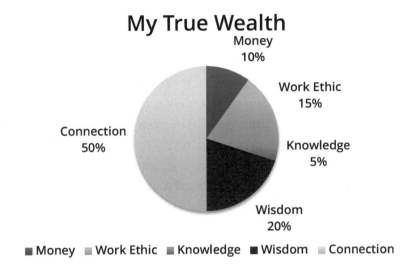

Over the next few chapters, I am going to introduce you to a non-traditional way I've learned to measure and safeguard true wealth. The first aspect I will dive into relates to the people in my life and how I get so much joy as a result of my shared experiences with them. That was not always the case. For many years, I struggled to find genuine human connection in my life. I used to think this was a "me" issue, but so many others have shared that same truth with me.

Do you struggle, too, with connecting deeply with people?

I have met so many businesspeople, sales professionals, and consultants who have struggled to attract new clients of high quality. Friends and neighbors who are parents, teachers, and coaches are, as I was, often baffled when the children, students, and athletes they love choose not to follow their lead. I have personally experienced and witnessed a major lack of human connection in recent times and a lot of confusion about why this is happening.

After twenty years of searching for answers, I learned the reasons I struggled to connect deeply with people:

As a lifelong helper, I was quick to offer an opinion, give advice, or make suggestions to help fix a problem. But upon closer inspection and a willingness to be completely honest with myself, I came to realize I was far too often giving this feedback before I had created an essential **trust** with whom I thought I was helping.

Here's how I started to see this all more clearly.

My business partner, Jim, is uniquely gifted at one specific thing. This is not something he's just good at or even great at, for that matter. It is his *unique ability* and it comes naturally to him. The funny thing is that, for much of his adult life, Jim was unaware of it. But once he became aware of it, he became obsessed with being the best at it.

Jim's unique ability is *establishing trust at lightning-fast speed and maintaining that trust for life*; real trust that starts with a series of intentional behaviors and is maintained and preserved for life by living by a simple set of principles. Within a profession of helping people navigate major life changes, nothing is more important than creating and maintaining trust.

> ***Creating trust and keeping trust are the most important skills to learn if you seek the power of human connection and a deep sense of personal wealth.***

Creating trust happens for Jim because he is able to quickly eliminate what he refers to as the "trust gap." To be a fly on the wall and watch Jim quickly eliminate a trust gap between a complete stranger and himself is a pretty cool experience. Although Jim was aware of his superpowers long before I entered his life, never had he taken the time to understand how he did it, nor did he care to.

What Jim *did* know was a total stranger would come into the office for a consultation and within an hour, was divulging deep personal hopes and fears the stranger had never shared with anyone. Within the course of a few hours, the stranger was hiring Gebhardt Group to help him navigate a major change in his life. What he also knew and quickly taught me was the results of having these trusted relationships left us feeling incredibly satisfied. A bit cliché perhaps, but these meaningful connections fed our souls on a level much greater than any financial success or accomplishment.

In my pre-Gebhardt Group days, I observed thousands of financial advisors interact with their clients and prospects over nearly twenty years—I had more than 15,000 hours of in-person research under my belt. Rarely had I seen in all of those advisor and prospective client interactions what I had witnessed in the conference room of Gebhardt Group. As I shared with Jim my observations, and how incredibly unique I thought this was, we both became deeply curious about *why* this was happening on a regular basis at Gebhardt Group.

Answers were soon to come. But what we knew then was these relationships brought so much joy and meaning to us that we wanted to better understand how it was happening. That way, we could possibly help others identify and create more of this major source of wealth in their lives, as we had in ours.

How was Jim creating trust so quickly? What was happening here that wasn't happening in most other places?

Ask. Listen. Feel.

Throughout most of this initial getting-to-know-one-another time with a prospective client, Jim did little talking, even after hearing the traditional "buying signs" that would signal an opportunity to close business. Instead, Jim would ask more questions.

For instance, one prospective client looked at her spouse in a meeting and said, "I'm not sure why we're keeping the money we inherited at the old brokerage." My previous training told me that sort of statement meant the couple only needed a subtle nudge to rehome their business. Yet, I watched as Jim glossed right by several opportunities to close the business. He persisted in asking questions, then listening intently and connecting with what the people sitting across from him were feeling as they got deeper and deeper into telling their story.

I discovered Jim's superpower of quickly **creating trust** is rooted in eliminating the trust gap between strangers and creating the foundation for true human connection. It happens as the result of properly flexing a misunderstood and often misused muscle in our body called *empathy*.

The word empathy is used a lot, but my experience is, when all is said and done, a lot more is often said than done. What I mean is people often talk about empathy, yet rarely practice it the way I witnessed Jim practice it on a daily basis in all areas of his life.

I think it may have something to do with the confusion of empathy with sympathy.

Here is the definition of empathy according to Merriam-Webster:

The action of understanding, being aware of, being sensitive to, and vicariously experiencing the feelings, thoughts, and experience of another of either the past or present without having the feelings, thoughts, and experience fully communicated in an objectively explicit manner; also: the capacity for this

Here is the definition of sympathy according to Merriam-Webster:

An affinity, association, or relationship between persons or things wherein whatever affects one similarly affects the other, mutual or parallel susceptibility or a condition brought about by it, unity or harmony in action or effect, inclination to think or feel alike, emotional or intellectual accord, feeling of loyalty, the act or capacity of entering into or sharing the feelings or interests of another, the feeling or mental state brought about by such sensitivity, the correlation existing between bodies capable of communicating their vibrational energy to one another through some medium

Let's try a self-check.

You speaking to me:
"Hi, how are you?"
Me responding to you:

"I couldn't sleep last night, and I haven't had an appetite all day. I almost got into a bad car accident yesterday and it has me really unsettled."

Your choice of responses:

a) "Oh man, I know how that feels. A jerk cut me off in traffic last week and it stuck with me for days."

b) "Sounds like a really big scare—I get why you haven't slept or eaten—you must feel awful."

Which statement is expressing empathy? Which statement is likely to foster more trust and a deeper connection?

If you selected (b) as empathy, you chose correctly.

The key difference between the sympathetic statement and the empathetic statement, is this:

Sympathy says, "I have felt what you feel." Empathy says, "I feel what you feel."

Do you notice the subtle difference?

Consider a more blatant difference I discovered in my interactions with people. My expressions of sympathy often came out like this: "I experienced that too and this is how I felt about it." Despite being sympathetic, it's a self-centered statement. Empathy, on the other hand, always came from thinking of others and trying to feel what they were feeling regardless of how I may have felt about the experience: "Sounds like you had a pretty big scare—that must have felt awful."

What I mean by this comparison is, if I sympathize with what you are feeling or experiencing, I make it about me and my feelings and experiences. If I empathize with you by feeling your feelings and validating them, then it's not about me; it's only about you. It's not to say that sympathy is a bad thing—it's just not nearly as effective at creating trust like empathy is.

Has it ever happened to you? A time when you felt truly understood because your thoughts and feelings were validated by someone? How did that make you feel? Safe? Connected? Maybe even loved?

Learning how to express empathy properly and selflessly has led me to believe that no other human expression has the power to move so much mass or carry as much weight.

Working side-by-side with Jim in various capacities since 2006, studying his unique ability, and witnessing the amount of influence he has on others, I now believe creating and maintaining trust is the number one "skill" required for maximizing one's impact on others and living a wealthy life. The key to establishing that trust is through the proper selfless expression of empathy. Whether you are a teacher, doctor, public employee, volunteer, parent, or garbage collector, being trustworthy is the greatest attractant to people around you and the most critical skill to develop if you seek the power of human connection. Empathy is the key to unlocking the door to a world of true wealth.

WHERE HAS ALL THE EMPATHY GONE?

Empathy requires listening skills. However, empathy is not a skill of just listening. It is a skill that requires you to feel others' feelings and connect with them at a molecular level.

Empathy, feeling what others feel without necessarily having the same experiences, is something we are born capable of expressing. But if you're like me, things in life happen and somewhere along the way we lose our desire to express empathy. I experienced plenty of my own pain and suffering. As a result, I inadvertently developed a hard, protective shell around my ability to feel what others felt in a misguided attempt to protect myself from more pain and suffering. I could still listen when others spoke, but because I had experienced a lot of pain myself, my desire and ability to feel others disappeared.

I often used to think to myself, "I've got my own problems, pal. I don't have capacity for yours, too!"

As a result of experiencing a lot of pain and hurt, I became self-centered and completely absorbed in my thoughts and views of the world—especially after my experiences of being bullied as a child. I learned to use my listening skills for self-serving opportunities. Or I would simply listen to think about what I would say next. My inner circle of close connections was miniscule, and my connection with most people outside my immediate circle had crumbled into the doldrums of small talk and self-interest; or as Jim likes to call it, "empty conversations about news, weather, and sports."

Empathy is still out there, but it's on the endangered species list. Its rarity puts human connection on life support. The lack of empathy between people is the greatest deficiency affecting human relations across the globe. Its lack is the main cause for so much pain and suffering in the world today. I would suggest that fear, greed, resentment, divorce, racism, poverty, war, obesity, ulcers, and every ounce of unnecessary hurt that exists could diminish if we exercised more empathy.

I propose to you that empathy is that powerful—more powerful at healing suffering than any humankind creation or invention *ever*.

If establishing trust is something you seek, and you are willing to become vulnerable by expressing empathy when in the presence of others, you are well on your way to having massive impact on others and tapping into the ultimate source of true wealth.

MAINTAINING TRUST OVER A LIFETIME

Maintaining trust is simple. It's not easy, however. Once trust is established, keeping it going for us has come down to adhering to five principles Jim and I like to call **Five to Thrive**.

I believe that everything we do in our personal and professional lives is guided by these five core principles. They are the North Star for us. They are specific but extremely broad when it comes to helping us make choices. They provide a directional for nearly every human decision we need to make that could affect another person.

We are far from perfect. But we have eliminated most of the rules society has imposed on us and substituted living by these principles to the best of our ability.
- Principle #1: Show up early and prepared
- Principle #2: Do what you say

- Principle #3: Finish what you start
- Principle #4: Say please, thank you, and you're welcome
- Principle #5: When you make mistakes, own them and fix them

PRINCIPLE #1: SHOW UP EARLY AND PREPARED

This is so much easier said than done. We live in an overscheduled, overwhelmed, and overcommitted society. We are perpetually late. I know I used to be. As a result, many people I know lack adequate preparation time for the commitments we say we're going to show up to. I have learned to use technology to help me show up early. Technology combined with discipline is the key critical piece. Being prepared is also dependent upon scheduling the time to prepare into my daily calendar and again, having the discipline to just do it.

PRINCIPLE #2: DO WHAT YOU SAY

So many people overpromise and underdeliver. I always used to. Trustworthy people do the opposite. They under promise and over deliver. So much of this has to do with our lack of ability to say no to people. We dive much deeper into giving ourselves permission to say no in Chapter 11 (Say No More). We will explore how saying "no" more helps us ultimately do what we say we are going to do.

PRINCIPLE #3: FINISH WHAT YOU START

How many unfinished home improvement projects are you in the middle of? Have you ever started writing a book, yet it sits unfinished? I started writing this book in 2014. It sat unfinished for a long time, despite publishing a shorter version of it in late 2015. As I learned to say "no" more often and to stay disciplined to a schedule, I found a greater capacity to finish the things I started. Only then did that feeling of accomplishment become my driving motivator going forward.

Principle #4: Say Please, Thank You, and You're Welcome

Gratitude is the cornerstone behavior of principle #4. It is as much a verb as it is a noun. What I mean by that is gratitude is an action that is expressed through words and behaviors.

Which one are you at the counter of your favorite burger joint?

    A. *"Gimme a cheeseburger, fries, and a chocolate shake."*
    B. *"I'll have a cheeseburger, fries, and a chocolate shake."*
    C. *"Can I get a cheeseburger, fries, and a chocolate shake?"*
    D. *"May I please have a cheeseburger, fries, and a chocolate shake?*

Which one are you when someone offers you thanks?

    A. *"It was nothing."*
    B. *"No worries."*
    C. *"Happy to do it."*
    D. *"You're welcome."*

How did you do on the quiz? There are no right or wrong answers. I try to live with as much gratitude as possible, and the smallest of things—like saying please, thank you, and you're welcome—are all part of small intentional behaviors that when put together, allow me an opportunity to spend a whole day in gratitude.

Principle #5: When You Make Mistakes, Own Them and Fix Them

Everyone messes up. Mistakes are some of our greatest assets if we are able to learn from them and improve upon them. Few people I meet own up to their mistakes or fix them. They simply choose to blame others. Mistakes serve as an opportunity to strengthen relationships when we can own them and fix them. Doing this is essential to maintaining trust.

Which way would you handle this mistake?

"Matt, you never sent me the report you promised me."

    A. *"Are you sure? I know I told my assistant to mail it to you. I'll get on her about getting it to you again."*

> B. *"I'm so sorry about that, Ms. Client. I told my assistant to mail it to you. Someone's head is going to roll over this."*
>
> C. *"I'm so sorry Ms. Client. I completely messed up on this one. I'll personally handle it immediately. What else can I do to make it right?"*

These five principles are certainly simple, but they are not easy to live by every day. By eliminating most rules I've been taught to follow and keeping the focus on these five things every day, I find success in my daily progress of improving myself personally and professionally. I can measure that by the growing number of people who rely upon me and count on me for safety—as someone they trust.

The amount of real wealth you create in life is a direct result of your ability to connect with other people, create trust, and maintain it.

I was born in 1972 with an obsession for challenging the status quo. I've lived nearly forty-seven years thumbing my nose at conventional thinking. I often make bold, provocative statements about what I see and experience around me. My cause for controversy is to help as many people as possible heal their broken relationships with money and people. If you're like I was, embroiled in a toxic relationship with money and personal finance that bled into your relationships with people, and you are seeking a solution to rebuilding your wealth one day at a time, this is where you start: connecting with people on a deep personal level by creating trust and fostering it with simple, repeatable role-model-like behavior going forward.

Like all worthwhile wealth-building ideas, this takes time, patience, and a lot of discipline. It will not happen overnight. I have rebuilt my wealth one relationship at a time by allowing myself to feel what others feel and by doing my best to live by Five to Thrive. This has been the epicenter of my ability to create real wealth in my life and I hope my experiences serve you well.

The Interfering Ego

In the last chapter, I introduced you to my experiences struggling to connect with others; how the pain and hurt I endured in my life led me to create this hard, protective shell on the outside. Once I learned this shell actually kept the pain inside me, I decided to go on an expedition to learn as much as I could about it. I spent a great deal of time dissecting and studying it so I could break down its walls and allow myself the gift that comes from real human connection. The shell is something I became intimately familiar with—the shell was my ego. For many years, my ego was in charge of most of my behavior, designed to protect me and keep me safe.

The first mystery I uncovered was my ego was not a one-size-fits-all phenomenon. For most of my life, I associated ego with a person who thinks highly of himself. It surely can manifest itself as narcissism, as it did so often in my life. But I've learned it can also be expressed in a variety of ways, such as fear, panic, anger, scarcity, comparison, gluttony, guilt, shame, and recklessness.

e·go / ˈēgō/ noun

a person's sense of self-esteem or self-importance; "a boost to my ego"

synonyms: self-esteem, self-importance, self-worth, self-respect, self-conceit, self-image, self-confidence; amour proper, "he needed a boost to his ego"

the part of the mind that mediates between the conscious and the unconscious and is responsible for reality testing and a sense of personal identity.

When we are fully aware of how our own ego shows up, we can transform it into a powerful ally who becomes beneficial to our survival when we are forced into fight or flight mode. But so many people go through life without this awareness of ego and how it works, thus remaining in a constant state of pain with adrenaline and cortisol pumping through their bodies all day long.

If unaware, ego tricks us into believing that its expressions are representations of our true self. It had me fooled for most of my life. This simply is not true.

Ego is really only our thoughts, and those thoughts can lead us to choose bad behavior, and an aware individual can certainly choose different behaviors in spite of those negative thoughts. Not only does this open the door for more peace and happiness, but it also just may save our lives.

My favorite source for studying my ego is the work done at the Enneagram Institute. The Enneagram Institute was formed in 1997 by Russ Hudson and the late Don Riso for further research and development of one of the most powerful and insightful tools for understanding ego types within ourselves and others: the Enneagram.

At its core, the Enneagram helps us to see ourselves and our egos at a deeper, more objective level and can be of invaluable assistance on our path to self-knowledge and connecting with others. I encourage you, if you have the desire to harness the power of real human connection, to explore this journey within and invest time with the wisdom of the Enneagram Institute, either by attending workshops or virtually through their website and online resources.

As I've learned more and more about my own ego, I've come to realize that my ego is actually run by a committee of voices inside my head; a cadre of actors, all clamoring at different times to be in charge. I was shocked to learn that there were a few different "selves" living inside me.

At first this thought of multiple voices in my head was complete insanity. I brought my concerns to my therapist and demanded that she have me tested for every mental disorder possible; schizophrenia, bi-polar disorder, depression, ADD, and whatever else she could come up with.

Instead, she helped me understand this was perfectly normal.

The thoughts and outward expressions I display to others can be extremely different and it does not necessarily mean I have a major illness to deal with. My therapist explained that my multiple thoughts, voices, and expressions represented unconscious "characters" inside the most primal part of my nervous system. That part of my brain that informs my controls, this thing called "ego."

I now know that not a single one of those actors' voices yelling at me and competing for my attention and action are the real me. They're my ego. The real me can't be seen, heard, smelled, touched, or thought about in any way—the real me is undetectable to the five physical senses I have. It can only be detected by the sixth sense; it can only be felt in a way that can best be described as an *intuitive knowing,* knowing it's there without any concrete physical evidence of appearing real.

The real me doesn't exist in my head; rather, he exists in my body, in my entire being. It's hard to describe the feeling when I know the real me is fully present. I guess the best way to describe it would be like the feeling I used to have back in my smoking and drinking days right after my first cigarette drag of the day, or after I downed my first martini of the night. It's a slight buzzy feeling throughout my body, except now I can access that feeling without putting cigarettes or alcohol in me. I can access that feeling by pausing and breathing, allowing the thoughts to move through my head as just that: thoughts. In just a few minutes of deep breathing, I feel that sense of "ahh." It's like a pleasant state of neutrality—I feel vulnerable but confident, pleasant but not excited. It's a peaceful feeling and that's about the only way I can describe, physically, how I know the real me has shown up.

To clarify more about what I'm suggesting, I'd like to introduce you to my actors, the cast of crazy characters that makes up the ego within my head.

Tommy Boy, My Wingman

Tommy Boy is a party animal at heart. For those readers who've seen the movie *Tommy Boy*, the character, Tommy Boy Callahan, played by Chris Farley, nails the actor inside of me.

My Tommy Boy always helped me deal with all obstacles by saying "fuck it." Tommy Boy is right there to tell me when something doesn't feel good or presents a challenge that won't be easy to overcome. That's when he thinks the fun should begin.

"Let's get drunk and stoned," he shouts. "It'll be awesome! And all those problems will go away. Once we're all messed up, let's see if we can find some real trouble to get into."

Tommy Boy was raging in my head the night of July 23, 2009. I was sixteen hours away from one of the most important presentations I have ever been asked to deliver. My audience was going to be in the range of several hundred to a thousand battered and beaten financial professionals. The Great Recession was gutting the innards of Wall Street balance sheets as well as the retirement accounts of most investors. I was a national spokesperson for a major insurance company. We were not only surviving the wreckage, we were thriving. Our firm had chosen not to take on the massive risk of leverage, credit default swaps, and other risky derivatives that so many other firms chose to take on. Professionals from across the financial services industry were looking to us for guidance.

I arrived in San Diego the afternoon of July 23, at the same annual industry conference I had to miss in 2005 due to my own personal Great Recession. Only, this time my own financial house was in order, as was that of my employer. I arrived carrying the weight of knowing I was going to have a room full of anxious financial advisors looking to me for hope on how to advise their clients while facing the greatest financial firestorm of our generation. Despite my own financial house being in good shape, I was still unaware of how my ego, specifically the voice of Tommy Boy, was capable of hijacking my response to stress, causing me to make bad choices that carried the possibility of life-changing consequences.

Much like I felt when I laid helpless on my bathroom floor four years earlier, convinced I was in the throes of death by cardiac arrest, I found my anxiety bubbling up from my chest ready to explode at any moment due to the pressure of the next morning's performance. Tommy Boy came racing to the rescue. As I sat in my hotel room the night before my big presentation, Tommy's famous words rang through my ears.

"Fuck this. Let's party!"

That was the relief I needed to hear. I was immediately dialing the mobile phone numbers of my colleagues who were also in town for the conference. Within minutes I had four friends rallied and ready for a night on the town. Although all four asked if it was wise for me to be out boozing it up the night before the big performance, Tommy Boy was running the show for me and he told them, "To hell with tomorrow. Tonight is about fun and celebration. When tomorrow arrives, we'll do what we do best." Do what we do best had become shorthand for winging it.

As the cocktails began to flow, the anxiety began to dissipate. As the night went on, the fun got even more fun. The Gaslamp district of San Diego is one of the world's hubs for party mania, and on that night, I felt like the host of the biggest party in town.

Dancing, drinking, eating, more drinking, yelling, laughing, we stumbled through Horton Plaza Park and the four of us wound up back in my hotel room wondering how we could keep the fun going. It was an epic night... until my friend Sean glanced down at his watch and looked at me as if he had just seen a ghost.

"Matt, what time do we need to be at the convention center to prep for your talk?" Sean asked.

"We're good—we don't have to be there until 7 o'clock tomorrow morning," I responded without concern.

"Dude. It's 6:30 in the morning. We have to be there in thirty minutes!" And like that, Tommy Boy disappeared like a genie being sucked back into his bottle, and all that was left was me, somewhere between drunk and hungover, trying to come to the realization of where I was supposed to be in thirty minutes.

After a quick shower and change of clothes, the four amigos hailed a taxi and arrived at the convention center ten minutes late. The same boss I had lied to about my reason for missing this conference in 2005 stood before me in complete disbelief.

"Matthew, do I need to find another speaker today?" John asked.

My eyes were bloodshot. My skin was pale. The smell of booze oozed through my pores.

"No, John. I've got this."

"You better, because if you mess this one up, consider your career with our firm over."

I swallowed with a hard gulp. I realized at that moment just how stupid my choice was to pull an all-nighter before the big show. Now my job was on the line. Add to that the responsibility of delivering hope to a beaten-down audience, and I knew the stakes were massive.

Despite my enormous hangover, I was determined to get on that stage and do my job. With an assist from four tablets of ibuprofen, a few liters of water, and a jug of eye drops, I was able to pull off the impossible. My hangover left me with no emotional space to feel the weight of my responsibility that day. I was able to hop onto the stage and pull off the performance of a lifetime, knowing whatever came out of my mouth was going to impact about 10,000 families that these 800 financial advisors in my audience were responsible for guiding.

I am not proud of the façade I projected that day. Despite succeeding in offering my audience hope for a secure tomorrow, I walked off the stage feeling like a swindler. Although my message was factually correct, my intent and my energy were fake. I carried a lot of shame, unable to face it or talk about it for a long time, even with my four amigos who were there to witness the impossible.

Despite the disgrace and the guilt over my all-night bender in San Diego in July of 2009, it took many more nights like this over the next eight years for me to realize how dangerous Tommy Boy was when he was in charge. I hadn't faced any legal problems or wound up in a ditch somewhere. But as a result of following the urges of Tommy Boy for as long as I did, I had nearly destroyed every close relationship I had. Tommy Boy had me running through people's lives like a tornado.

At 11:45 p.m. on January 20, 2017, after a night of drinks and sushi with my few remaining friends, I ordered one more cocktail: a dirty vodka martini on the rocks with three olives. I took two gulps, put it down on the bar and walked out. I haven't had a drink since.

Giving up alcohol was one of the best decisions I have ever made. I have no regrets over that decision as it has given me an opportunity to mend the broken relationships in my life. It was the catalyst that finally helped me quiet the voice of Tommy Boy inside my head.

Sometimes I think about how impossible it was that Tommy Boy had not gotten me or someone else killed. It is almost beyond belief. Tommy Boy still exists inside my ego. But I've finally been able to tell him to go sit in the corner and shut up when he tries to mutter in my ear. He can still occasionally trick me into eating too much or staying home from the gym. But he's no longer in the way of me staying sober, helping others, and keeping my own financial house in order. There was a time when I truly loved to engage Tommy Boy. He still shouts in my ear almost every day, but it has become my choice to never act on his advice ever again. Instead of listening to Tommy when my nerves bring him out of hiding, I find someone to connect with. I get out of my head by diving into someone's heart.

VINNY, MY VICTIM

Vinny whines to me almost every day. He's constantly complaining how the world is unfair and how everyone else has it better than we do. He is a victim of bullying and lashes out like a grizzly bear when he senses anything that reminds him of our childhood. He blames the world for mistreating us and never seems content. Vinny never accepts blame and cannot own his misperceptions of the world. Like Tommy, when he shows up now, I find someone else to turn my attention to. I get away from Vinny by connecting with others.

In 2011, I was the coach of my son Lucas's Little League team. I was responsible for herding thirteen little eight-year-old boys two afternoons a week and most Saturdays throughout the spring.

One warm Saturday before a game, one of my coaches was pitching whiffle balls to all the boys as they stood in a circle, swinging wildly at every ball that came their way. One of those pitched whiffle balls came screaming off a bat and landed squarely in the face of one of the little boys on the team named Tyler. Ironically the assistant coach who was pitching was his dad. Tyler immediately began to cry. I offered him help and escorted him to his mother on the sidelines. His dad smiled and resumed pitching whiffles to the circle of boys.

Tyler's cheek was a little red from the sting of the plastic whiffle ball. Tyler's mom met us with a slight chuckle.

"Oh, you poor thing," she said with a smile. "Coach Matt, can you please give Tyler an ice pack?"

I only had one ice pack in my first aid kit, and I knew this little hot spot on Tyler's face was nothing more than a slight skin irritation from the smack of the plastic ball.

I responded to Tyler's mom, "Can you take Tyler to the bathroom and put a cool cloth on his face? I only have one ice pack and I want to save that for a more serious injury."

You can't make up what happened next.

Tyler's mom morphed before my eyes. Her smile mechanically twisted into an angry robotic looking scowl. Her body shifted and began moving in odd jerky motions. Her mouth opened and she began belting loud enough for everyone on the field to hear her.

"Are you fucking kidding me? You're not going to give my son your fucking ice pack?" She berated me, inches from my face, her index finger deeply planted in my chest. I was stunned by her outburst.

After ten minutes of ear-piercing obscenities, she stormed off with her son, supposedly never to be seen again by anyone on my team. The parents in the stands all surrounded me in disbelief over what had just transpired. Even Tyler's dad, my assistant coach, came over to my side, apologizing for his wife's eruption.

He shook my hand and said, "Don't worry about her. She gets mad like that. Just give her a few days to cool off and all will be forgotten."

Within a week of Tyler's dad apologizing on behalf of his wife for her reaction, I was summoned by the board of directors of my Little League. They had received a harsh letter from both of Tyler's parents, demanding I be removed from my position as a coach.

Yes, the dad who just a week earlier shook my hand apologetically, co-authored this letter.

In the letter, they referred to me as a child abuser for failing to give their son my last remaining ice pack. They also wrote that I had verbally abused Tyler's mom.

A child abuser and a woman abuser?

Vinny the victim was ready to attack.

The board grilled me about what had transpired on the field that day. Based on my account and that of twelve other families who witnessed the tirade, the board concluded I made a dumb decision by not giving up my last ice pack. But they did not find me to be a child abuser or a woman abuser who was incapable of coaching children.

Vinny the victim was still angry, but at least he felt exonerated after that board meeting.

When the board of directors informed Tyler's parents of their decision, they responded with threats of lawsuits. An all-out war broke out between Tyler's parents and the board of directors, who were now defending my character as a respected long-time coach in the league.

After a few weeks of back and forth written communication, it seemed as though Tyler's parents were going away quietly in defeat. Our baseball season continued without Tyler and his family. The season ended in June and life resumed after Little League baseball.

It was a cool October night, months after the drama of the Little League season had passed. I was sitting at home, playing on my new laptop, preparing for meetings that upcoming week. Google was becoming popular and I decided to search for my own name just to see what might pop up.

The first item to come up was a website:

www.mattgrishmanabusedmyson.com

Yup, you read it right. Matt Grishman Abused My Son dot com. I was horrified; this had to be a sick joke.

I clicked the hyperlink. What I saw made my chest feel like it was going to explode. There was a full-blown website dedicated to me, painting me as a vicious child abuser who needed to be publicly shamed for predatory behavior.

A picture of me was front and center. In the picture I appeared as a Nazi Gestapo, my face tackily Photoshopped over a picture of Tom Cruise as a Nazi officer in the movie *Valkyrie*. Being Jewish, I was bewildered by this imagery.

Below this dreadful doppelgänger was my name, address, and phone number for all the internet to see. Below my contact information in bold red font, the site read:

City of Rocklin residents:
We must stop this child abuser before he hurts another child

Vinny the Victim came blaring through me. It took maybe three seconds for him to take over my entire psyche. I yelled out for my Amie to come see what I had just found. We knew immediately who was responsible for creating this website.

"I'm going to kill them both," I said in a complete state of insanity. I ran to my bedroom, grabbed my car keys and my wooden baseball bat and marched to my front door.

Amie gulped and asked, "Where are you going?"

"I'm gonna deal with this right now." I was bursting at the seams, tears running down my face, overwhelmed with anger. Amie ran down to the front door and threw herself in front of me, blocking my exit.

"Don't do this," she pleaded.

"I have to. No one attacks our family like this and gets away with it." I was blind with rage. Vinny the Victim was in full grizzly mode.

But Amie would not step aside. She knew I was not thinking clearly, that I could hurt people at worst, and that even a best-case scenario if I left the house would have a bad outcome. Her defiance was all the stall tactic necessary to keep me from leaving the house and doing something I would later regret.

Within a few minutes of Amie pleading with me to breathe and come back upstairs, I felt the anger slowly fade from my face. My heart rate began to slow, and my thoughts became clearer. As Vinny the Victim faded back into the depths of my ego and the real me reappeared, I was able to sit quietly for a moment. I started to cry again.

I called my close friend and attorney, Marshall. I told him what I had found online.

"Matthew, this is simply awful," Marshall said. "I will contact the DA's office first thing in the morning and see what we can do to have this site shut down. The reality is, some of this is protected under their First Amendment right to free speech. However, they cannot post your contact information on this website encouraging the community to contact you. That can be considered harassment, which is against the law. Whatever happens, I will handle the legal end of this for you."

"Thank you, Marshall. Can you please also begin drawing up a lawsuit for defamation of character or slander or libel or something?" I desperately asked.

"I can, but is that really what you want to do? You will spend tens of thousands of dollars in legal costs and, even if you win a decision, chances are they'll never pay you. Is that really worth the amount of money and energy that will consume your life, only to come up empty in the end?"

Marshall's next statement rocked my world.

"How much punishment do you really need to inflict upon them? Isn't it enough punishment for them to have to live this way, with this much anger and hatred in their hearts? It appears to me there's nothing you could do to them financially that would hurt them more than the way they live right now."

Marshall was right. The victim in me wanted revenge. But the truth was, no amount of retribution could punish them more than how they must have felt every day of their lives. They were stuck living a life of hell on earth. No one with that much anger and hatred could ever truly feel a sense of love and joy.

Thanks to Marshall's efforts, a month after the discovery of the website, my contact info had been removed. Amie reminded me, if the website were going to remain active, there was nothing more we could do about it. People who knew me would not believe what it said. And those who didn't know me and passed judgment because of the website were likely not people I was going to associate with anyway. Amie reminded me about all the hatred people like politicians and television personalities received daily in the tabloids. They learned to ignore it.

The oldest childhood saying became my mantra for the moment:

"Sticks and stones may break my bones, but names can never hurt me."

Even if the "names" were put on full display on the world wide web!

As word of this website began to spread throughout my circle of friends and acquaintances, Amie's wisdom proved true. One of my supporters decided to create another website to detract internet traffic from the abuser site. His site, www.mattgrishmaninspiredmyson.com, was an exact replica of the offensive one, only its message was as the URL suggested. Within weeks of publishing the new site, the abuser site began to slide way down in the Google search of my name.

By the start of the next Little League season, the site claiming I was an abuser of women and children was permanently removed. I guess it wasn't getting the results the creators had hoped for, and the cost of maintenance had become too great.

Vinny the Victim almost caused me to behave in a way that could have resulted in me serving a lengthy prison sentence. I still occasionally struggle to this day to shut him up. As I become more aware of Vinny the Victim and his voice in my ego, I can choose to let his voice fade to the background, much like I have with Tommy Boy.

I now completely dislike the idea of being a victim. I've learned through this experience that nothing in life happens to me; instead, everything happens for me. This experience taught me the power of forgiveness and compassion for others. As outrageous as that entire experience was, all because I was too stubborn to give up an ice pack, I have long since forgiven myself for my mistake. I have forgiven that family and no longer carry the weight of resentment toward them. I felt like twenty pounds had been lifted off of my shoulders the day I actually felt forgiveness toward them.

Sadly, I didn't encounter this family again for many years, and in less than desirable circumstances. I received a call about a recent widow who was going through a major life transition after losing her husband. She was referred to me by a colleague who knew we specialized in helping people endure these circumstances. It was Tyler's mom. Her husband, my former assistant coach, was diagnosed with an aggressive form of leukemia and died in 2017. Of all the wealth advisors in my community, it would just so happen she would wind up being referred to me.

Captain Corporate, my CEO

I met this guy for the first time in the summer of 2016, when I was meeting with my accountant to review my progress on my continued fiscal growth. Captain showed up with a grand entrance, and since meeting him, he is constantly in my head, demanding I stay productive. He is the driver in my head who kicks my ass when Vinny is trying to run the show. "Stop whining and coming up with excuses and justifications. Just do what you need to do. Own your shit and fix it."

As my accountant challenged my relationship with money, questioning whether I was in the midst of a relapse to my old ways and whether I was willing to do whatever it took to get my financial house in order again, Captain Corporate lashed out at him. In not so many words, he said, "Fuck you, Glen. I've got this." Captain is the ultimate hardhead and is the one voice responsible for keeping me in charge of everything, despite the lessons I've learned about how I am not in charge of anything. I am grateful for his presence, as he keeps me focused and on track. But, if I let him, he'll keep me stuck in my head and unable to connect with others in the present moment.

MATTY, MY PEACEKEEPER

Matty is a gentle voice who speaks to me on occasion. He is always happy and in love with everyone we meet. But I have learned that his intention to give away love is filled with conditions; primarily the condition that we receive love back. He'll occasionally raise his voice when I'm about to speak the truth, especially when that truth may hurt someone's feelings.

A therapist might call Matty the co-dependent part of my ego, meaning much of my emotional well-being over my life has been based on the emotions of others; especially when it comes to the people closest to me, like Amie, my boys, and my parents. Matty says my happiness depends on their happiness. I've particularly subscribed to the old cliché that a happy wife equals a happy life. It's taken me most of my adult years to come to a place where I could recognize Matty's voice inside my mind and choose not to act on his co-dependent needs. When I get out of my head and into someone else's heart, I find I don't need others to like me or be happy with me for me to be okay.

SAUL, MY SKEPTIC

Saul is an even newer actor inside me. I realize he's always been there, but my wingman and best party pal, Tommy Boy, has always had an overpowering voice of optimism and pleasure-seeking that never quieted long enough for me to hear Saul. Since I silenced Tommy Boy in 2017, Saul has begun to speak up. He speaks to me now almost daily, questioning every decision I make; questioning the credibility of every person I meet.

I've come to appreciate his protective ways. I know he just wants to keep me from getting in trouble, but sometimes he's a real downer.

Saul thinks everyone is looking to take advantage of me, even if it's a person who is crying out in desperation for my help. When I blindly listen to Saul, I find myself closing my mind and my heart to opportunities to help people. I have to work hard to quiet Saul now. But, like Vinny the Victim, once I recognize Saul's impulses, I can successfully redirect myself by being with someone else in the present moment, be it in person, by picking up the phone and calling someone, or by simply sending someone a text to inquire about his or her day.

Separating from My Actors to Find the Epicenter of Connection

The stories I've shared about the characters in my head are some of the extreme examples of how allowing my ego to dictate my behavior led me down dangerous and dark paths. And even today, these voices still exist. However, they all now serve a much different purpose—I now have the power to choose differently from what my ego wants.

Are you wondering how you can separate from the constant chatter of your mind, find some quiet, make better choices in the moment, and become able to truly be present and connected with others?

In the next section of this chapter, I'm going to share with you how I was able to do it, how I was able to get out of my head and into someone else's heart. For those who have done the hard work and can learn to separate their true self from their ego, the gift of human connection comes hard and fast. It is a feeling that can only be described as experiencing heaven on earth. It is a feeling greater than any feeling money has brought into my life. It is utter joy and bliss.

First, I must offer full disclosure and share with you my intent. By no means am I suggesting that my path is the only path to empathy and harnessing the power of human connection. All I am offering is how I found my ability to connect deeply with people and create meaningful, authentic relationships with those I meet. Should you find another path, I would be eager to hear your story and how you did it. This is simply how I did it.

QUIETING THE NOISE OF EGO
WITH A POWER SOURCE I DON'T UNDERSTAND

Prior to embracing the power of human connection, I spent most of my life irritable, restless, or discontent, especially when people, places, or things weren't as I would have liked them to be. The actors in my head turned me into a control freak who had to be in charge of everything. It was no small task for me to learn how to accept things as they were; in effect, accept life on life's terms. For me to acquire this level of acceptance about others I had to start with a willingness to believe in a power in the universe that was much greater than me and the actors in my head, a power that was, in fact, not a human form.

Although I had sworn off religion and God at a young age, I always knew deep down that something spiritual was out there. Something that could be an explanation for the unexplainable. I just never knew how to access it. But to truly connect with others and accept them as they were, I knew I needed to quiet the actors in my head and tap into this higher power I knew little about.

Since I had little understanding of this seedling of spirituality that was developing inside me, I decided to call it "Big Brother."

Why Big Brother? I knew I didn't need a higher power that was like a father-figure or another boss (I've had both of those already in my life). What I needed was more of a big brother in my life; something or someone that would look out for me without judging; that could guide my thinking and help me get away from my ego and the actors when they wanted to be in charge; that helped me think more of others and how I could be of service to them. It also required me to realize I had little control over my ego and the thoughts it created in my mind.

To design my own spiritual relationship allowed me to really believe in it.

For me, Big Brother has become a presence in my life that is loving, comforting, and all-knowing. He looks out for me and he's there whenever I need him: twenty-four hours a day, seven days a week. He even works on holidays and weekends!

Please allow me to be impossible to misunderstand. My spiritual relationship with Big Brother has nothing to do with religion or any specific religious beliefs. For some people, joining a formal religious organization, attending church or a synagogue, and knowing God as he is taught to you by others can prove helpful in dealing with life and connecting with others. I do not judge those who do seek religion as their spiritual foundation, nor do I judge those who call themselves atheists or agnostics. For me, religion was not the answer. I was a lifelong atheist who swore off religion at a very young age.

My relationship with Big Brother came from a desire to think of others more than I think of myself, and this was next to impossible for me to do with all the self-centered chatter going on in my head. Too many years had been spent getting through my day, looking forward to the weekend, always drowning in thoughts of regrets for my past and fear for my future. For me this pattern was not sustainable, yet what I wanted seemed unattainable. I wanted to have impact, and I wanted that impact on others to give my life meaning. From that meaning would be my happiness. There was no way I was ever going to have impact if I was left to my own thoughts, regrets, and fears.

My relationship with Big Brother came from a foundational belief within me that we are all connected as one, that all living things are of equal importance. We are all expressions of this beautiful creation called life and not one of us is more important or worthier of love and life than another. As a human I had come to believe our primary purpose is to love one another and to put others ahead of ourselves for the greater good. These were not always my beliefs, but these are my spiritual beliefs now, and they are attached to me at a molecular level.

To find this required me to do a few things every day:

1. I thank Big Brother every morning for giving me another day to help people.

2. Throughout the day, I ask for Big Brother's guidance, then quiet myself to listen. Sometimes answers don't come right away, but when I'm diligent about asking, they eventually do come, through my thoughts or through other people. How do I know they're messages

from Big Brother and not the actors that make up my ego? Simple: When the messages or thoughts have nothing to do with me, I know they're from him. When my thoughts are about me, I know they're from one of the actors in my head.

3. Finally, when I go to bed at night, I review my day and take note of any instances where my ego was in charge that day. Where in my day was I gluttonous, angry, fearful, or dishonest? Do I owe anyone an apology? If I do, I make sure it's one of the first things I do in the morning after waking up and thanking Big Brother for another day to have positive impact on others.

I am not suggesting that my beliefs are to be your beliefs or to serve as your understanding of your Higher Power. I'm simply offering my path as an example of the type of relationship with a Higher Power one can develop if understanding ego, expressing empathy, and truly connecting with others is what you seek.

The Higher Power I have in my life now is the Big Brother I always wanted when I was growing up. He comforts me and helps me make better choices when feelings like anger, fear, and resentment creep into my mind. Rather than reacting impulsively to these destructive thoughts, I close my eyes, take several deep breaths, and ask Big Brother to help me find peace and serenity. Within a few minutes, the anger, fear, and resentment subside. I thank Big Brother for the assistance, as now I can get back to doing what I truly love: connecting with people.

I was recently in the car with my youngest son, Lucas. Just before this, I had gotten into a heated disagreement with my wife. Traffic was awful and, to make a frustrating moment worse, we got stuck at a railroad intersection with a freight train that was crawling at a snail's pace. I felt my anger beginning to rise up through my body and into my face. I began swearing out loud and tapping my foot with impatience. I had somewhere to be, dammit! I started pounding away on my smartphone looking for alternative routes away from this time-waster of a railroad crossing. After a few seconds, I recognized the anger boiling within me and how destructive it would become if I let it continue. I made a conscious choice to close my eyes, begin some deep breathing, ask Big Brother for a little help, and then listen. Sure enough, help arrived. Within a minute or so, the anger slipped back down my body and vanished. A smile came over my face, and I opened my eyes to see my beautiful teenage son sitting next to me making silly faces. We spent the next eight minutes as the train crept by singing to the music on the radio, holding hands, and laughing at how crazy I looked when I was pissed off. Then our laughter shifted to how horrible my crackling voice sounded compared to Beyoncé's voice pumping through the speakers. That little intervention with Big Brother turned a wasted moment of anger and resentment into eight extra minutes of love and connection with my son.

For those who choose to develop a relationship with a Higher Power and an awareness of ego, the ability to truly connect with others is granted almost instantly. It takes daily practice, but as we learn how to use our empathetic abilities, others genuinely sense the shift within us; a shift from self to others is unmistakably authentic and refreshing.

Empathy is a feeling that has no describable action. As intuitive beings, we sense when real empathy is being offered. It becomes the key ingredient to trusting others. Once that trust is established, then an "action" can be given and received. This action is what I refer to as offering compassion. Or, in my world of financial advice and relationship coaching, compassion becomes the action of offering solutions to problems; and no solution is more effective than one offered from a compassionate space; even if it's advice or a solution that may not be what my client wants to hear. Without establishing empathy and the trust that follows, solutions and advice will always fall on deaf ears.

I have found this to be the singular reason most business people, sales professionals, and consultants fail to convert prospects to clients, or why parents, teachers, and coaches fail to connect with children. They offer advice or solutions to problems before the trust gap has been completely eliminated.

Our clients almost always take our advice or are at least open to discussing the solutions we have presented. So are our children. When the rare occasion occurs where they do not, we re-examine where we went wrong. Where did we miss our opportunity to eliminate the trust gap? Did we get in our own heads too much and think too much about ourselves? We go through an inventory of our own behaviors rather than blaming our clients or our children for being pig-headed or short-sighted.

As my empathy muscle has strengthened (thanks in large part to my relationships with Jim and Big Brother) the quality of my relationships has improved exponentially, both personally and professionally.

These relationships are built on a real sense of trust and mutual respect. They are based completely on love. Barring a major change of heart, they will last my entire lifetime.

This can be the focus of your most impactful work! Once you get out of your own head, become aware of ego, and develop a relationship with a power greater than yourself to help you separate from ego, your ability to create trust at lightning-fast speed will give you the greatest power in the universe: The Power of Human Connection.

It's pretty simple to find this power, but do not mistake simplicity for ease. You must devote yourself to daily practices and commit to stop chasing recognition, money, power, and prestige.

Cat's in the Cradle

My dad is one of my heroes.

I am proud to be the son of Henry Grishman. From the time I was a young boy, I wanted to spend every minute I could with him. I wanted to dress like he dressed. I wanted to talk like he talked. I wanted to inspire people the way he did. I wanted to be able to fix things like he fixed them. I wanted to be him.

My dad is a driven career-man, aspiring to be the best at what he does. As I sit and write this book, he is the school superintendent of the number one rated public-school district in America according to Newsweek magazine. He has inspired thousands of young adults to go after their dreams and become meaningful contributors to society as doctors, scientists, teachers, accountants, wealth advisors, Nobel laureates, and more. My dad's impact on our society has been massive.

So much of my childhood played out like Harry Chapin's lyrics to "Cat's in the Cradle." I was proud of my dad, and no matter how busy he was, I never gave up hope that soon he would have time to play.

My child arrived just the other day.
He came to the world in the usual way.
But there were planes to catch, and bills to pay...

Chapin's immortal song stuck with me for years, and as I got older and graduated college, career prospects started coming my way.

In 1997, I was offered an opportunity to relocate to the West Coast to represent a world-class asset manager.

The race was on.

Within two years of moving to Seattle, I found myself with a "1K" membership with United Airlines, an honor bestowed to the company's exclusive 100,000-miles-a-year travelers. The counter ladies at the Hertz Gold desks up and down the West Coast knew my smile and my first name. I had built my own fast-paced career and, like my dad, became a father myself.

Initially, my dad and mom would come to visit us religiously every six weeks. But as my miles in the sky increased and the demands of twenty-first-century parenting took my weekends from one Little League game to the next, the visits became fewer. By the time I was thirty-five years old, my professional life had me in high demand Monday through Friday, and as the father of two little boys, I was in high demand at home too.

I cherish what I learned from my father as I grew up watching him become the best in his business. He taught me a huge lesson in the value of following one's true purpose and developing the belief that you can transform the lives of many people. As a result, I have become a dedicated coach, both for my boys and for my clients. I was put on this earth to challenge the status quo and teach others how to do the same. I'm obsessed with it.

Fortunately for me, I also get to express my purpose through my daily interactions with my boys, teaching them about life and how to be a transformative figure themselves, and how to go completely counter to the culture. Most of this learning happened through the great game of baseball. I never cared much about the scoreboard and whether the team won or lost in the eyes of our spectators. My boys learned that going counter to the culture required them to show up for baseball focused, grateful, confident, and ready to give it their all.

My schedule has become so full between my business and my boys, that I now find that I have less time to spend with my dad.

> *And as I hung up the phone, it occurred to me,*
> *He'd grown up just like me.*
> *My boy was just like me.*

Every year, my dad, brother, and I meet in Las Vegas for a wonderful long weekend.

We put aside our careers and our lives at home to just be with each other. We eat like royals and play a little craps in our favorite casino. We walk up and down the strip, people-watching and taking in all the wonders of Las Vegas. But the most important thing we do while we're together is talk. We talk about life, love, experiences, and chasing our dreams. It is three days each year I am grateful for having. Although I often wonder what life would have been like if I had been able to spend more time with my dad growing up, I realize the time I had with him was exactly the way it was supposed to be. It helped me realize my true purpose and gave me the courage to live it out. It's also allowed me to consciously choose the relationship I have with my own sons. The time I have with my dad now is priceless, and I am truly grateful for it.

This, to me, is a huge measure of true wealth. I am a wealthy man because of the people in my life and the time we get to spend together.

Thank you, Dad, for teaching me these important lessons in building wealth:
- Cherish the time and experiences you have with those you love
- Go out in the world and be the best at what you do
- Have the most impact you possibly can
- Never give up

I love you more than you could ever imagine!

What I Learned from Pa

On November 17, 2011, my father-in-law, Alan "Pa" Lanzendorf, lost a long battle with pulmonary fibrosis and I lost one of the greatest teachers I had ever known. Since then, I have spent a great amount of time reflecting on our twenty-one years together and all the things I learned from his amazing life and remarkable stories.

Pa was a brilliant man. At sixteen years old he entered Tufts University in Massachusetts. But since his dad only had enough money to pay for two years of college, Pa was forced to drop out and join the Army. After an honorable discharge, Pa returned to college on the GI Bill and earned his degree from Syracuse University in 1957. He dreamed of being a park ranger in one of our most beautiful national parks like Yosemite or Yellowstone.

Truly, Pa could have been anything he wanted to be, whether a military officer, doctor, lawyer, or a rocket scientist. But Pa chose a different path. He fell in love with being a husband and a father, and that's all that mattered to him. Pa took a nine-to-five job as an analyst for the Department of Criminal Justice for the state of New York. It became a thirty-five-year career that allowed him to be home every night for dinner and participate in all things family-related. Pa never traveled for work. He never interrupted his family time to take a call from his boss.

Money was never Pa's passion, yet he always seemed to have enough. His wife, Carol, was dedicated to caring for their four kids. Together they created a warm, safe home with food on the table, clothes on everyone's backs, and top-notch college educations for their children.

Pa was also a man of devout faith, and it was really the simple things that he enjoyed most. Pa believed in God, and every Sunday he put on his best suit and attended church. He told me countless stories of Boy Scout camping with his boys and the Sunday drives the family took after church. As he got older, his greatest joy came from walks with Carol, reading his newspaper, playing on the floor with his grandkids, and having long philosophical talks with just about anyone willing.

I was one of the lucky ones who spent hours in conversation with Pa, listening to the stories of his life, amazing people he met, and personal difficulties he overcame. Yet, despite the challenges that would have made most people resentful in life, Pa always treated others with incredible kindness and compassion. Whether with family or a complete stranger, Pa was genuinely interested in people, and they knew it from the minute he said hello. He expressed empathy unlike anyone else I had ever known. He was a truly gentle, loving soul.

Pa was one of the wealthiest men I ever met. He was never rich in worldly goods, but he was grounded in his love for his family, the simplicity of his fun, his ability to connect with others, and the work ethic he carried for nearly forty years.

This wealth is the most valuable inheritance he could have ever left for me.

In my role as a wealth advisor, I meet many financially rich people who are completely broke when it comes to true wealth. Many tortured souls arrive in my office with more money than most people could spend in eight lifetimes, yet they are unhappy at work, they are at odds with their spouses, their kids are often a mess, and they feel completely stuck. What I inherited from Pa has helped me connect deeply with people like this and help them begin to heal their strained relationships with money and the people they love most.

I am incredibly grateful every day for the work we do in our business, helping people identify, strengthen and protect their true wealth . . . not just their financial riches.

The Core Values of True Wealth

Family

The foundation of true wealth is family. This is not exclusive to relationships by blood. For the most part, you get to choose whom you call family. These people give you a deep sense of **connection**.

Who are the most important people in your life? Identify them. Cherish them. Offer them devotion, compassion, and forgiveness. These are the people who bring great energy into your life. Your relationship has transcended any situation or circumstance that may have brought you together in the first place, like at work, church, youth sports, etc. These are the people you love unconditionally—you have their back no matter what and they've got yours.

Occupation

What is your true ***purpose***? How do you give your gifts to your community and the world? Do you work, volunteer, coach? I have learned to believe in the power of giving and receiving. Identifying what inspires you to contribute to your community is a critical part of measuring one's true wealth. It has been said that the two most important days of your life are the day you are born and the day you realize why.

Recreation

How do you like to have ***fun***? People we meet ultimately realize simple things generate the most fun, especially if these activities involve the people you care most about. Family vacations, walks, family movie nights, dinners out with friends, and weekend ball games are all things clients tell us are their favorite fun things to do, and none of them require a lot of money to be enjoyable.

Money

What is your belief system surrounding money? Are your most important personal values aligned with how you use your money? Does your relationship with money give you a sense of ***financial security***? I meet people with lots of money who tell me they earn plenty of income but don't know where it all goes. Others spend a lot of time and energy preparing their estate for their children, yet they do not spend an equal amount of time preparing their children for the estate; they are unaware their estate will likely be squandered quickly on meaningless "stuff."

Have you measured your true wealth?

True wealth means so much more than having lots of money or making a large salary. True wealth is measured by the integration of your core values—your relationship with family, occupation, recreation, and money. Having complete clarity here can allow for greater fulfillment and joy in life.

I have dedicated my life to helping families identify, honor, and pass on their true wealth. This is the greatest gift I received from Pa, and I am forever grateful to be able to share this gift with others in need.

Pa would want it no other way.

Teach Your Children

In 1970, Graham Nash wrote the song *Teach Your Children*. His struggles with his own father inspired him to produce a piece of music that evokes real emotion for almost everyone who hears it. Nash said about the song:

> *"The idea is that you write something so personal that every single person on the planet can relate to it. Once it's there on vinyl it unfolds, outwards, so that it applies to almost any situation."*

In 2005, I found myself in a do-or-die financial firestorm. I had become the picture-perfect definition of the hypocritical, reckless spendthrift whose career was to lecture others about money management. It was the low point in my financial life. I woke up every day in a cold sweat, embarrassed at my failures, living in constant fear that I would lose my job, my home, and my family. I relied on alcohol every day just to find some relief. I hated myself.

I eventually realized I was at the bottom, and that I could make the difficult choices to right my financial ship. This was no small task, requiring the help of several advisors to help me stay accountable for making better choices. My impulsiveness was overwhelming, as was my self-loathing and my drinking. Beginning my journey forward required me to meet weekly with my therapist, Lani. She helped me learn to forgive myself for the disaster I had created around me. We'd spend weeks of couch time becoming aware of the triggers in my life that would encourage my impulsiveness.

With time, growing awareness, some new spiritual beliefs, and a great deal of discipline, our weekly talks became weekly celebrations of mini-achievements. I reined in my spending and actually began to save. By forgiving myself and surrounding myself with the right people, I found myself in a much different financial position just six years after hitting bottom.

After escaping the clutches of corporate America in 2011, I chose to make it my purpose in life to help others own their financial mistakes, fix them, and pass those invaluable lessons onto their children. Whether your bills are paid in full at the end of every month, or you stretched a little too far to buy a vacation home and a fancy car, or you must do some hocus pocus to make ends meet, there's a good chance you have some less-than-perfect money habits. These habits can have a profound effect on your children, just as mine did.

Despite what you may be thinking, your not-so-perfect money habits can serve an incredible purpose, and ultimately be one of the greatest gifts you ever give your children.

What are *your* bad money habits? What are your good habits? What money habits did you inherit from your parents, good or bad? What habits will you commit to changing for good, starting now?

Many young adults lack basic knowledge of how to balance a monthly budget or save for their future. Many are assuming massive debt with car loans and student loans, some without a clear vision of how to repay these debts. They are not necessarily taught the basic principles of simple vs. compound interest, and how debt can cost them significantly over their lifetime. Public schools and universities have done a better job in increasing exposure to financial education; however, these efforts must be supported by good financial "home-schooling." The theories and opinions learned in a personal finance class cannot compare to witnessing and learning from the practical choices, mistakes, and real-life money decisions kids see their parents make at home.

THE POTENTIAL FOR PARENTS AS TEACHERS

From a young age, many children pay attention to how money is treated in their home. Many parents are missing the opportunity to use these observations as teaching opportunities. Most parents I meet tell me they prefer not to say anything when there are struggles or disagreements about money, especially with things such as debt, paying for college, monthly budgeting, and family income. They believe they're protecting their kids from their mistakes.

This can't be further from the truth, however. My experience, personally and in working with others, has taught me that parents who make significant money mistakes and involve their kids in learning from those mistakes see their kids carry those lessons (and resulting smart choices) into adulthood. While many studies and articles address this phenomenon, the strongest case for this argument is that the overwhelming majority of millennials (those born between the mid-1980s and the early 2000s) despise debt. People might think their kids don't know about the $20,000 credit card balance Mom and Dad have, but they do. Kids are perceptive. If Mom and Dad are secretly fighting about money, the kids know about it.

Practicing hypocrisy and lecturing kids about perfect choices with money can drive them to more compulsive, destructive money behaviors. The fear I initially see from parents in speaking the truth is that their child will be their little copycat, making the same mistakes they have made. However, my experience has been quite the opposite. I have found our kids and my clients' kids are making wiser choices with their money because of our honesty about our own mistakes and subsequent lessons.

Some basic things we can all teach our kids (based on mistakes I have made over the years) are how to:

• Balance a checkbook or reconcile an online checking account.
• Budget each month for things like electronic devices, new clothes, or fun with friends.

- Value experiences with their friends rather than the relentless pursuit of acquiring meaningless stuff.
- Give back and allocate a portion of their money to a cause greater than themselves.

I suggest parents take thorough money inventory. Write down your money mistakes, past and present, and what those experiences have taught you. Share these with your kids. It's an exercise with multiple benefits. First, it forces you to sit and become honest with yourself about where you may have mismanaged your finances. Awareness is the first step toward choosing a new path. Second, it allows you to become vulnerable and authentic in your relationship with your child, deepening their respect for you, and showing that a true leader owns his or her mistakes and works hard at fixing them. That's a priceless life lesson.

Finally, you can begin to prepare your kids for your estate and your legacy by teaching them to talk openly about financial blunders. Children need permission to make mistakes and develop the belief that mistakes can become our most valuable assets.

Here are a few suggestions on how to share your mistakes and the lessons learned from them with your children:

Own your mistakes and devote yourself to fixing them.

First things first: forgive yourself for not being perfect with money. We are all flawed and that's okay. If the best time to become a great steward of your money was twenty years ago, then the next best time is right now. Become aware of your mistakes, own them by writing them down, and be willing to fix them. If you don't know the best habits for using credit cards or how to make a household budget, seek professional help through a financial planner or tax planner, and learn with your child.

Create a family spending plan.

Most families I meet earn a healthy living, yet they often tell me they don't know where the money went at the end of the month. Spending everything you make—or, even worse, spending more than you make—is a certain path toward insurmountable debt and poor lessons for the kids.

Consider setting a weekly or monthly family budget meeting.

Sunday nights after dinner is a great time for everyone to sit down and review the family bills and upcoming expenses for the week. This way the kids can see exactly what it costs on a weekly basis to manage the household finances.

If you're like most parents, you probably hear things from your kids like, "Dad, why can't I buy a new iPhone for $800? Everyone in my class has one but me."

An exercise in weekly family budget planning can provide a quick and understandable answer that puts the kibosh on it, once and for all. It's also okay to explain to your children that you are a family that stands for something bigger than buying stuff.

Be willing to admit when you make mistakes with your weekly budgeting by overspending on unnecessary items. Be open in discussing what you could do better as a family.

Save, no matter what.

Not everyone believes they can afford to save. I encourage clients to read *The Richest Man in Babylon* by George Clason so they can learn the most important wealth building lesson of all: the first person to get paid every pay period is *you*.

Ten percent of your take-home income should go into savings before any bills get paid, even if this is as little as $10 per paycheck (more on this later in the book). It is critical to teach your kids the importance of investing in themselves and paying themselves before they pay anyone else. Ideally, your savings should include an emergency cash fund as well as a fund for your retirement, like a 401(k) or an IRA.

Protect your credit.

Almost everyone I know has debt: mortgage, car, student, and/or credit card debt. Debt has become part of the fiber of America. You as a parent must step up and show your children how important it is to properly manage and protect their credit. Even if you struggle to pay your outstanding debt, paying something is better than ignoring it.

If you are at a point where you have gotten in a little over your head with debt, involve your children in a discussion about how you got to this point and about handling your responsibilities going forward. Then call those you owe and make manageable payment arrangements with a timetable of when your debt will be paid off. It's an incredible lesson to teach your kids: Sometimes we just must deal with cleaning up financial mistakes, no matter how hard it is.

Agree to disagree

Disagreements about money can be some of the most damaging dynamics in a family environment. I meet families all the time who have different priorities when it comes to money. In February of 2018, Dave Ramsey released a study called "Money, Marriage, and Communication." In his research, Dave found money is the number one culprit for causing disharmony in a marriage. Dave claimed the majority of couples who got married in the past five years started off their marriage in debt, which has been a direct cause for unhappiness and disagreement.

It's no wonder so many families battle over financial issues, but it doesn't have to be that way. In our private wealth management practice at Gebhardt Group, Inc., we encourage families to sit and have discussions about differing views on money. Where do we agree?

Where do we struggle to agree? Can we truly listen to one another's values and work to support each other despite our differences?

Finding common ground with money is not an easy exercise, and families who have a hard time tackling it should seek professional help. This is some of the most important work we do in our business.

I've shared my mistakes with my children, and their financial habits are better because of them. My oldest son saved his money to buy his first car and have spending money for college. My younger son saves his money for online gaming and nights out with friends; nonetheless, they've both learned an important lesson in valuing money and the meaningful experiences it can buy you if you treat it with respect.

As parents, there's nothing we want more than for our children to do better than we have in life. Helping them learn from our mistakes is a big part of the process.

> *Teach your children well.*
> *Their father's hell did slowly go by.*
> *And feed them on your dreams.*
> *The one they pick's, the one you'll know by.*

Realistic Expectations vs. Unrealistic Demands

Are you constantly irritated by a tardy co-worker? Are your teenage kids driving you nuts because they never seem to pick up after themselves? Does it bother you that your boss is nit-picky about the stupidest things? Are you unsatisfied with the returns you get on your retirement account compared to everyone you talk to? Do you often demand better than what you get?

If you answered yes to any of these questions, you may have some expectations that are really unrealistic demands.

If you find yourself feeling restless, irritable or discontent with others failing to meet your expectations, you have two choices: continue to expect they change their behavior or learn how to adjust your expectations. One choice will likely result in continued irritation. The other will eliminate your daily discontent.

I know what you might be thinking. How can this guy expect me to accept anything less than excellence in those around me? It's not my job to change . . . it's theirs! That was my reaction the first time it was suggested that I adjust my expectations of others. I get it. But what I eventually realized is that *demanding* excellence and setting *realistic expectations* of excellence are two different things.

Here are three tips to help you begin to eliminate demands and set realistic expectations.

Tip #1: Determine the Control Factor.

To determine whether an expectation is realistic, look at how much control you have over the matter at hand.

Can you control the return on your retirement fund? Can you make your co-worker be on time for team meetings? Can you make your teenager pick up his mess? The answer to these questions is a resounding "no." I guess you could withhold allowance or iPhone privileges to force your teenager into cleaning up after himself, but he can still choose not to do it despite the consequences.

To have an expectation based on something entirely outside your control only sets you up for frustration and letdown. If you have little to no control over the outcome you expect, you have set an unreasonable demand rather than a reasonable expectation.

Tip #2: Take the History Test.

Let's pick on my teenage son again.

For fifteen years I lived with constant frustration, especially during my son's middle school years. He could never seem to keep his room clean. He never seemed to turn his homework in on time. And he copped an attitude when I nagged him about either or both. Our father/son relationship was deteriorating rapidly until someone I trust asked me a magical question that woke me up to my reality as a parent of a teenager.

"Why do you expect your son to clean his room and handle his schoolwork today when he never has before?"

That was the moment I chose not to expect that my son's room would be clean or that his homework would be turned in on time. I just let it go. Now I shut his door so I do not have to see his messy room. The byproduct of eliminating this unreasonable demand is that I'm not as angry as I used to be, and my son and I get along better because of it. When he does clean his room or meet schoolwork deadlines, I am pleasantly surprised and I get to shower him with praise.

Coincidence?

We used to spend entire weekends angry at each other. He was frustrated at himself for being mindless with his schoolwork, and I was mad at him for it. Now, we enjoy our weekends and my son has found the motivation and freedom to be more mindful of his cleanliness around the house. Even more important, he is turning in his work and getting better grades. The effect this modification of my expectations has had on the overall happiness in our family is felt daily.

The takeaway is this: If history tells you one thing, demanding a different outcome in the future is unrealistic. It's bordering insanity.

Tip #3: Stop Staring at the Horizon—Measure your Progress in Arears

Although we have discussed setting realistic expectations for others, doing this can only happen if you set realistic expectations for yourself.

Do you feel unhappy with your professional progress? Do you feel like you should be further along in your career? Do you feel frustrated with the lack of retirement savings you have accumulated? Do you get mad at yourself when you're late for a meeting? Do you demand yourself to be a better person?

I have met many people in my life, and I have yet to come across the perfect person.

Yet so many people I know demand perfection from themselves. It's what they've come to expect. You might be one of them.

When was the last time you made a mistake and were okay with it? Really okay with it? If you're like most of us, you kick yourself inwardly and then find yourself yelling at your kids an hour later for doing the same thing.

How do we set realistic expectations for ourselves? We often look at the horizon and compare where we think we should be to where we are now, whether it is at work, in our retirement savings, or in our overall happiness in life.

But the horizon is not a realistic place to set expectations, because you can never reach it. Rather, we should spend more time looking at history (remember Tip #2) to see how far we have actually come. You will be amazed at your progress when you take that historical perspective, instead of feeling constant disappointment over failing to meet your own expectations by looking at a far and distant horizon.

Repeat after me: "I give myself permission to make mistakes."

Say this over and over. Setting realistic expectations for others starts with setting them for yourself.

As a business owner, of course, it would be ludicrous for me to not have a high standard of excellence. So how can I *expect* excellence without *demanding* it? As an example, I expect excellence from our operations specialist, whom I hired in 2015. How?

First, I get to choose whom I will invite to join our team. Control factor: Check!

Second, I have worked closely with this person for ten years in volunteer capacities. After watching her work ethic, her attention to detail, and her belief that perfect is better than done, I knew she was the right fit for Gebhardt Group, Inc. The history test: Check!

Third, despite expecting excellence, I also know there will be mistakes along the way. Acknowledging this still allows me to believe in and expect excellence in those I choose to have around me.

I believe it's okay to make mistakes, as long as you own them and fix them. Allow yourself to be imperfect and set reasonable expectations for yourself. Really. Once you have done this, you will be equipped with the tips in this chapter to set realistic expectations for others. The benefit to you will be much more peace and much less irritation in your everyday life. I promise!

(By the way, I have no expectation that you will actually change your demands of yourself and others—see the proceeding for that "control" factor!)

Say No More

Your happiness and desire to have positive impact on others are directly connected to your ability to **say no more** and **say no, more**. It's a little play on words that offers a way to begin moving toward a life of abundant wealth, joy and meaning.

For the past twenty years, I have been obsessed with studying the lives of the wealthiest people on earth; from famous heads of state, to Main Street, USA families. Some of my subjects had more money than one could spend in twenty lifetimes. Others barely had two nickels to rub together their entire life, yet they made a massive impact. Despite some sizable economic differences, my subjects all possessed the same basic belief structure when it came to defining the key components to True Wealth. To the naked eye, all of my subjects radiated wealth. Only by looking at personal net worth statements would one notice anything different between them.

One of the key critical pieces that linked every one of these wealthy people was their uncanny ability to **say "No."** They developed this ability because they all chose being happy over being right.

In our private practice, my business partner and I counsel families on how to build healthy relationships with their money and each other. This often begins with helping clients make a choice between being right and being happy, or, another way to look at it, we help them decide to chase the desire for recognition or the desire to impact others. Then we introduce our favorite little two-letter word. It has become a critical key step within our financial planning process, the

Wealth F.O.R.M.ation Experience ™. To help them get started, I share my own story of how, after obsessing over how truly wealthy people lived happy, meaningful lives, I transitioned from wanting recognition to wanting to have impact. This is what I tell them:

Say "No," More

Prior to adopting this mindset of wealthy living, I was the model "yes-man." If someone asked me to do something or be somewhere, I said yes without even thinking or considering the impact it might have on my wife and children. When it came to volunteering at local schools, in my community, as a mentor, and at just about any organization I was a part of, I said yes every time. If it needed to get done, you could count on me!

Some might say this was a good thing, being so giving of myself to others. But upon deep reflection, when forced to be completely honest with myself, I wasn't doing it to be of service to others. I did it so everyone would offer me kindness, consideration, and endless amounts of praise for my hard work.

Under the façade of helping others, I was able to get attention and recognition. But it left me exhausted and at odds with the people I was closest to. My obligations at home started to slip. Paying my bills on time became a rare occurrence. Returning my mom's phone calls, being present for my family, running my business, maintaining my own health, and doing the things I knew truly made me happy all fell to the back burner. I wanted to be liked. I wanted to be recognized. I wanted to be right. But none of this was giving me a sustained feeing of joy. The only time I thought I was happy was during the anticipation of a pat on the back. Within a few minutes, I was miserable again, right back to my nonstop pursuit of 'atta-boys and affirmations. I reached bottom when I looked around and realized I was standing all alone. The people who meant the most in my life wanted little to do with me. I was on the verge of losing everything and everyone who mattered.

Today, I live a very wealthy, joyous and meaningful life. I spend no time trying to convince others I'm worthy of recognition. I only offer suggestions when others ask. I have no attachment to the outcome of my suggestions. I have also learned to say no to anything that doesn't serve my true purpose, which I now know is *waking up every day with gratitude, challenging all forms of conventional thinking, and offering up my unique set of skills and talents for the benefit of others.*

This shift from being recognized to having impact was profound. It required me to finally give myself permission to say no. My first few attempts failed. But once I was underway, I got hooked. The feeling that **saying "no," more** gave me is indescribable, but I'll do my best by sharing how I did it.

I started by saying no to the little things I had previously always said yes to; daily Starbucks runs, checking emails after 6 p.m., and other stuff I called my **baby nos**. The **no's** gradually became larger; I was able to **say "no," more** to being the first to volunteer at the Little League park, going to parties, taking on clients who would not take my advice, and spending time with people who sucked the life out of me.

I recognized **saying "no," more** to these things allowed me to **say "YES," more** to the people and things that really fed my soul and gave me energy. I felt the burden of being overwhelmed peel off of me like a wet wool sweater. I was enjoying every day of the week, whether I was at work or at home—even Mondays. I knew I was getting close to something very special, but there seemed to be a few weighty, less obvious things that I still needed to **say "no" to more**.

Finally, it hit me; eleven more things to which I needed to **say "no," more** if I were going to live a truly happy, impactful life. I chose...

- **no more** complaining
- **no more** excuses
- **no more** gossip
- **no more** limiting beliefs or "I can't"
- **no more** playing victim
- **no more** self-loathing
- **no more** dwelling on the past
- **no more** fearing failure

- **no more** resisting change
- **no more** tolerating mediocrity
- **no more** accepting the status quo

These eleven new **no's** seemed simple, but they have not been easy. I am far from perfecting my ability to **say "no," more** but with every day of practice I see exponential progress.

When I feel like **(1) complaining**, I simply pause and breathe. After a summer of devastating Atlantic hurricanes and mass shootings, I am reminded quite quickly that there is never anything in my privileged life worth complaining about.

When I feel the need to make up an **(2) excuse** for why I can't do something, I pause and go counter to my thinking. I tell myself that I *must* do that "something." I fight through the resistance that's trying to get in my way via these excuses of my ego and I persist forward.

When others try to engage me in **(3) gossip** or any discussion about other people, I have learned to say, *"Well, I'm not sure about you, but that falls under the category of none of my business."* Then I usually walk away, since it serves no one to speak about others when they are not present.

When my mind blurts out *"you can't"* because of a **(4) limiting belief**, I once again pause. When my boys come to me with an outrageous idea by most people's standards, like *"Dad, I want to fly the space shuttle, cure cancer, and pitch the winning game 7 in a World Series with the New York Mets,"* I tell them to go for it with all they've got. Maybe, just maybe, if they know I believe in them and that they can accomplish anything they're willing to work for, they might actually do it!

If I perceive a wrong has been done to me, I refuse to **(5) play the victim.** In my quest for being recognized, I played a victim role worthy of an Oscar. It never served me well. It kept me angry and resentful. Now I know that I am responsible for how I react to others and how I feel inside; no one else is. If someone tries to hurt me intentionally, there's no need for retribution or feeling as if I had been victimized. That unfortunate soul has to live inside his or her evil skin—that's punishment enough. I certainly don't need the toxicity of victimhood on top of it.

When I screw up, which I do every day, I refuse to allocate any time to attending my own pity party. I don't **(6) self-loathe**. It doesn't serve me, and it doesn't serve those who depend upon me. I forgive myself and know deep in my heart that my mistakes are the greatest learning opportunities I have in life. This goes hand in hand with **(7) dwelling on the past** and **(8) fearing failure**. Any time I dwell on past mistakes or find myself fearing future failure, I pause and think of one of my favorite little sayings: *"Today was the tomorrow I was afraid of yesterday."* It's pretty ridiculous when you say that out loud, isn't it? I can't change what's happened. I can't predict what will happen. Any time I spend saying YES to those thoughts is really me **saying "no," more** to what's happening right now.

Finally, **(9) resisting change, (10) tolerating mediocrity, and (11) accepting the status quo** have been the exact reasons my life and my level of happiness seemed to never improve—funny how that works. There's another favorite saying I learned: *"If nothing changes, then nothing changes."*

What I am sharing here is a choice I have made based on my observations of the wealthiest people I know. It's a simple choice, really, but not an easy one to make. For me, living with a mindset of being recognized by others came at the cost of having real impact on others and being happy. I was missing the joyousness around me. I was wasting the gifts I was put on this earth to give to others by saying "yes" to everything that could help me get recognition. I was on a path to dying young, angry, and resentful.

Saying "no," more became the prescription I needed to find the joy and meaning my life was meant to have. The feeling is powerful and it's right there if you truly want it.

Part III

My Relationship with Money
BUILDING AND PROTECTING FINANCIAL WEALTH

Getting Started on the Right Path

Whether you're just getting started as a young adult and want to build your wealth the right way, or you're like me and you've had it, lost it, and are now looking for the discipline to rebuild it all over again, choices must be made to kick off a lifelong journey of important financial decisions.

For young adults, it starts with finding that first full-time job and choosing the right mix of corporate benefits like health insurance, disability insurance, group life insurance, and retirement accounts. Next comes purchasing a car, making a down payment on a first home, getting married and having kids, and ultimately saving for college so your kids can earn a degree of their own.

For those who are just beginning, the decisions of financial adulthood may seem daunting. This may count double for those who have tried and failed, and who are looking to hit the reset button. Take heart: financial sobriety and making responsible decisions with your money that support your true wealth is all possible, even if you are starting over.

It starts with securing full-time employment and leveraging some smart behaviors with the income you create and the benefits you are eligible for through that employment.

TIP #1: PAY YOURSELF FIRST.

Rule number one is to make sure you budget every month to pay yourself first. Before rent, car payments, utility bills, or cell phone bills, set aside 10 percent of your gross paycheck in a savings account that is dedicated toward helping you become a better "you."

This money is not for a new iPhone or a big-screen TV. It could be, however, for taking an online graduate class, a gym membership, or new work outfits.

Regardless of how you choose to "invest in you," always remember that *you are your own greatest asset*. You must learn to set aside funds to help you continue to improve your skills, your health, your image, and your opportunities.

TIP #2: CREATE YOUR RAINY-DAY FUND.

After setting aside 10 percent to invest in your future you, your next 10 percent must be deducted for a rainy day or emergency fun.

A study by Bankrate.com showed more than 60 percent of Americans have virtually no savings set aside in an emergency fund. As you take on more and more financial obligations (such as car payment, mortgage, and student loan debt), the risk of running into unexpected financial troubles increases. To protect yourself from the inevitable, create another savings account, separate from your "pay yourself first" account, which allows you to build a cash cushion for the unexpected.[1]

By saving another 10 percent of your income every month, you'll be able to accumulate a few months of salary before you know it. Before you even consider purchasing your first home, it is wise to have at least three months of salary set aside for emergencies if you're single, or six months of salary if you're married with children.

TIP #3: BUY HEALTH INSURANCE.

Many healthy workers are tempted to skip enrolling in a health insurance plan to pocket more of their paychecks.

---

[1] Adrian Garcia. Bankrate.com. January 2019. "Survey: Most Americans Wouldn't Cover $1,000 Emergency with Savings."
https://www.bankrate.com/banking/savings/financial-security-january-2019/

Consider health insurance one more investment in you. Remember, you are your most important asset. Health insurance for a healthy worker is cheap compared to basic medical care. One day in the emergency room can cost tens of thousands of dollars. A recent study estimates that 66.5 percent of personal bankruptcies are related to medical debts, so it's critical to budget for insurance so you can avoid adding to that horrifying statistic.[2]

TIP #4: CONTRIBUTE TO A COMPANY-SPONSORED RETIREMENT PLAN OR A ROTH IRA.

Most eighteen- to twenty-five-year-olds have difficulty thinking about an obligation forty days from now, let alone planning for a retirement forty years in the future. But the sooner young people start saving for retirement, the better off they'll be come retirement. The same holds true for people in their thirties, forties, and fifties. The best time to start preparing for retirement is very early, but the second-best time is today.

Most employers offer some sort of pre-tax savings tool to help you set the groundwork for retirement; this is usually called a retirement, deferred compensation, 401(k), 403(b), or 457 plan. Even if you do not have this benefit at work, you can contribute up to $5,500 per year into an individual retirement account (IRA), or, even better, a Roth IRA.

A traditional IRA allows you to defer paying taxes on the growth of your account until retirement. The Roth IRA, however, allows you to withdraw funds tax-free from your account as long as you follow rules regarding Roth IRAs.

It's important to remember that whatever you save in a retirement account or IRA is meant for your retirement and should not be considered savings for a rainy day. Anything you withdraw from these accounts prior to age fifty-nine-and-one-half will be taxed heavily—

---

[2] Lorie Konish. CNBC. Feb. 11, 2019. "This is the real reason most Americans file for bankruptcy."
https://www.cnbc.com/2019/02/11/this-is-the-real-reason-most-americans-file-for-bankruptcy.html

you will have to pay both your ordinary income tax rate, as well as a premature withdrawal penalty of 10 percent.

Start early and think of your retirement savings as a gift from your younger self to your older self. Despite the temptation to ignore retirement until you are older, starting now makes a huge difference.

Let's look at an example.

Allison and John are both twenty-five and make the same income. Allison decides to begin saving for retirement and starts funding her retirement with $458 per month ($5,500 per year) with pre-tax money. At age forty, after fifteen years of contributions, Allison stops.

John decides to delay saving for retirement until he feels a bit more financially secure. At age forty, he starts funding his retirement with the same amount as Allison—$458 per month—until he retires at age sixty-five.

• Allison's fifteen years of contributing $5,500 per year (from age twenty-five to forty), will total $82,500 contributed.

• John's twenty-five years of contributing $5,500 per year (from age forty to sixty-five), will total $137,500 contributed.

Assuming a 6 percent average annual rate of return, Allison will have $582,402 accumulated in her retirement by the time she reaches age sixty-five. But by the time John turns sixty-five, he will have only $319,860 in his retirement.

Starting Early: Compound Interest at Work

	Age during contribution	# of years contributing	Total contributed	Total value at age 65
Allison	25-40	15	$82,500	$582,402
John	40-65	25	$137,500	$319,860

*This example assumes 6 percent average annual rate of return—does not reflect taxes, fees, or the effect of market losses

That's a huge difference! Even though Allison will fund her retirement at $5,500 per year and stop when she turns forty, she will have already accumulated $135,699 in her account, which will continue to earn an average annual rate of return of 6 percent per year through age sixty-five. With just the earnings on her retirement balance, and no additional contributions to the plan for twenty-five years, Allison's retirement nest egg will be more than $250,000 greater than John's.

John will have contributed more to his retirement than Allison, even though Allison still ends up with far more money.

As a side note, if Allison were to continue contributing $5,500 per year until she was fifty-five, then $6,500 a year from fifty-five to sixty-five due to the catch-up provisions in the IRA laws, she would accumulate almost $1,000,000 in her IRA.

In addition to starting early, keep in mind that many employers also offer a retirement "match." This means that they will match a certain percentage of your contributions to the plan. Most often, companies match up to 3 to 6 percent of your income. If you make $50,000 and contribute 10 percent ($5,000) of your income to your retirement, your company could potentially add as much as another $3,000 a year on your behalf.

By not contributing the minimum amount to get a potential employer match, you're throwing away the opportunity to earn free retirement money. Start saving at least 6 percent of your paycheck every pay period in your retirement account—I typically recommend 10 percent, depending on your situation—and continue to increase your percentage every year until you hit the maximum amount you can save ($19,000 in 2019).[3]

If you happen to be like me, starting over with retirement saving, some time is better than no time. In other words, don't give up hope just because you're in your forties or fifties. The best time to prepare is when you're starting out, but the second-best time is today.

---

[3] Lorie Konish. CNBC. Nov. 2, 2018. "Here's how much you can sock away toward retirement in 2019."
https://www.cnbc.com/2018/11/01/heres-how-much-you-can-sock-away-toward-retirement-in-2019.html

Tip #5: Treat Your Personal Balance Sheet Like a Business.

I hate to state the obvious, but it never hurts to remind people to spend less than they earn. It's a critical habit to start now. Run your personal balance sheet like you are a business. A business cannot be successful if it spends more than it earns. Neither can an individual.

Creating a businesslike balance sheet for your personal finances is not as difficult as you might think. Start with writing down how much you earn (gross wages) on a blank sheet of paper. Below your gross wages, subtract 10 percent to pay yourself first. Add a second line for your "rainy day fund" and subtract another 10 percent for contributions to that account.

Next, account for payroll deductions like federal and state income taxes, FICA (Social Security and Medicare), health insurance, and retirement contributions. Since these are automatically done for you by your payroll department, simply record them on your balance sheet directly under your 10 percent profit distribution. After you have accounted for these initial deductions from your gross income, you now have a remaining balance for your monthly expenses.

Here's the crucial part of running your personal finances like a business: Do not spend more than you have in this remaining balance.

Your finished balance sheet should look something like this:

Total Monthly Income	$5,000
Profit Distribution	$500
Emergency Fund	$500
Taxes	$750
FICA	$250
Health Insurance	$250
Retirement	$500
Remaining Balance for Expenses	$2,250

The balance of $2,250 is now what you have to manage your monthly expenses, including rent, utilities, car payments, cell phone bills, food, and entertaining.

TIP #6: PROTECT YOUR CREDIT.

Learning how to use credit at a young age is an important life skill. Although you should never spend more than you make, learning the proper way to handle credit is a key component to running your personal balance sheet like a successful business.

Begin by opening a credit card at your local bank with a modest spending limit. Make a few purchases each month and pay off the bill in full. This will help build credit and good borrowing habits, both of which you will need to buy your first house.

It's like an athlete building muscle memory. Once you create the discipline to pay your credit card bill every month, it becomes a lifelong habit that simply happens automatically. Building this muscle starts by remembering a credit card is not a license to buy what you cannot afford. You must learn the discipline of paying your balances off every month and budgeting properly. To pay interest on an expensive dinner or new watch is not a smart use of your capital, or your credit.

This may sound like a lecture you have heard before, titled "Do as I Say, Not as I Do." Well, it is exactly that. I tell you this from my own personal pain . . . the incredible pain of regret. By the time I was thirty years old, I had accrued over $100,000 in credit card and consumer debt. What I had to show for all that wasted spending was very little. Sure, I owned two Rolex watches and a nice German car. But most of the time, the watches sat on my night table collecting dust, and by the time the car was paid for, it ran like an old jalopy.

The mountain of credit card debt left me with little memory of the fancy dinners or new outfits I had acquired. There was no greater feeling of failure than to have reached the pinnacle of my professional career only to realize I had maxed out all my available credit by purchasing meaningless stuff, and then be left with no purchasing power to manage a family crisis (or even put gas in my car).

Tip #7: Spend meaningfully.

Despite all these money-saving tips, the idea of spending money and having fun is okay. After all, this is your life we're talking about, and life should be fun. But at the risk of sounding a bit too philosophical, is a new iPhone every year or $15 a day in lattes really what you want to remember most about life after college?

If you've created a solid financial budget, there's nothing wrong with spending some money. Just consider using it on things that will create great lifelong memories of the people and places that matter the most to you. A weekly dinner out with good friends, a backpacking trip through Europe with your old college roommate, a cross-country drive with your BFF . . . these are all things you will look back on as memories worth the money spent.

Binge on experiences, not gadgets that will be obsolete in a year.

A simple guide for spending is to follow the 10-10-10 rule. It basically goes like this: how will you feel about a purchase or an expense in ten weeks, ten months, and ten years? If the expense will be meaningless in ten weeks, skip it; you can certainly live without it. If the purchase will have a lasting effect in ten weeks but won't roll your socks up and down in ten months, consider delaying it until you come across some extra money. If the expense will still have you talking about it ten years from now, go for it without hesitation.

Tip #8: Accept that you do not know everything.

Don't be shy about asking for help when you're unsure . . . and I'm not talking about asking Siri.

If you're young and inexperienced, ask your dad about his first car purchase, and then ask for his advice. Ask your friends what they pay in rent. Ask your mom for an introduction to her financial advisor to help you with your retirement options. Get an introduction to a trusted accountant to talk about your taxes.

We now live in a digital age where everything you wanted to know is in the palm of your hand, thanks to Google. But it's important to know there are no universal truths to money and saving for the future. Not even the internet can provide all the right answers. What may be good advice for your neighbor may not be good advice for you. There is no online digital substitution for in-person, custom advice, and the help is out there for you.

All you need to do is recognize you don't have all the answers and ask for help.

Middle School Math Finally Pays Off

Did you know there is a simple formula, something you likely learned in middle school, for calculating your potential wealth?

It all starts with a little temptation and curiosity.

Have you ever wondered how long it would take to double your money? Believe it or not, you can figure it out pretty easily; hence the middle school math reference. I briefly mentioned this formula a few chapters ago, but it's well worth repeating in much more detail.

According to the Stern School of Business at New York University, since 1928, stocks have averaged about 11 percent return per year; bonds have averaged about 5 percent per year, and cash has averaged about 1 percent per year, although according to a 2018 report by Bankrate.com,[2] the average money market rate in America was 0.21 percent. It's important to know that these are long-term averages, and rarely do these investments actually return their exact average in any given year—nor does anyone actually hold an investment for over 90 years! Investing requires patience and understanding that in any given year, your actual return could fluctuate considerably above or below the average long-term return quoted above.[4]

In fact, the stock market has only returned its average (between 10-11 percent) three times since 1928 (10.81 percent in 1968, 9.97 percent in 1993, and 10.74 percent in 2004). That's only three out of eighty-

---

[4] New York University. January 5, 2019. "Annual returns on Stock, T.Bonds and T.Bills:1928-Current."
http://pages.stern.nyu.edu/~adamodar/New_Home_Page/datafile/histretSP.html

seven years! The remaining eighty-four years have delivered returns much greater or much less than that 10 to 11 percent average.[5]

Why is this information so important to calculating one's future wealth? It all boils down to a simple formula called "The Rule of 72." The Rule of 72 is a mathematical certainty that says if you take 72 and divide it by your annual average return, your answer will yield exactly how long it takes to double your money.

Let's use our examples from above:

- 72 divided by a 1 percent money market return equals a 72-year double of your money
- 72 divided by a 5 percent average return on your bond portfolio equals a 14.4-year double of your money
- 72 divided by a 10 percent average return on your stock or stock mutual funds equals a 7.2-year double of your money

In other words, using our example, one dollar invested in stocks would be worth two dollars in 7.2 years. This becomes especially important when you factor inflation into the dialogue. Long-term inflation (or the rising cost of stuff) has historically been about 3 percent. Although current inflation is low, most financial professionals recommend factoring in a 3 percent inflation rate when planning for your retirement as a margin of safety for your future spending needs.

If the price of stuff increases by 3 percent per year, that means the price of stuff doubles about every twenty-four years. This makes sense if you simply look at the price increases in a U.S. postage stamp. In 1990, a stamp cost a quarter. Twenty-five years later, the price had increased to 49 cents, nearly doubling in cost. What this means for us, the retirement savers of the world, is our money may need to grow at a rate better than inflation if we plan to purchase the same things in retirement that we do today. Since some expenses like college tuition, food, and health care are inflating at a rate much higher than 3 percent, many of us may need to have a portion of our retirement exposed to

---

[5] Bankrate. June 10, 2018. "8 Best Money Market Accounts for June 2019." https://www.bankrate.com/banking/money-market/rates/

higher-return potentials, like those that can come from owning stocks or mutual funds—assuming we can tolerate the added market risk this will bring, along with the potential for losses.

The Rule of 72 is a helpful little math formula that can offer you a bit more clarity in what lies ahead for retirement and all future known (and unknown) expenses.

In the coming chapters we will have a discussion about a variety of different tools available to you to accelerate your ability to save for future needs; whether that be a rainy-day fund for emergencies, a down payment on a first or second home, assets to pay for college expenses, or a flush retirement savings account to replace your working income one day when you're ready to retire.

One of the most important things I've ever learned about creating wealth is that it is *my responsibility to create my own wealth*. It's not up to my stockbroker or insurance agent or real estate agent or banker or financial advisor; it's up to me. My ability to have a lot of financial wealth is primarily based on my capacity to earn money and save more of it than I spend. I have yet to find a get-rich-quick strategy that can apply to the masses, nor have I found a crystal ball that can identify the next Google or Apple for me to invest $1,000 in today and have it wind up being worth $10,000,000 when I sell my shares to the public. Creating wealth takes time and it takes a great deal of discipline.

Generally, people I meet create that wealth by starting with a job. They start a business or work for someone else. They become experts at their craft. They are financially rewarded for their expertise. Eventually they show up in my office looking for advice on how to protect what they have created and seek an effective way for making that wealth work for them over the rest of their lives.

Once they've begun saving and putting aside money from their job or business, people can enhance and protect that wealth through the various vehicles, tools, and products we are about to discuss in the next several chapters.

There is often a great deal of misinformation and misunderstanding of what these tools can do and how they are best used as a method of enhancing and protecting the wealth you have created. I'd like to help clear up some of that misinformation.

But before we take the plunge into learning about these various tools, what is your first feeling when I say the following words?

STOCKS. BONDS. MUTUAL FUNDS. EXCHANGE-TRADED FUNDS. ANNUITIES. LIFE INSURANCE.

Many people have very strong feelings about each of these types of products and sometimes just saying the word evokes an emotion.

- I say *stocks* and people often break out in fear of losing all of their money because of what they, or someone close to them experienced owning stocks in times like the Great Recession of 2008 to 2009.
- I say *bonds* and people often stifle yawns. Bonds are so boring!
- I say *mutual funds* or *exchange-traded funds* and people sometimes just look at me confused; as if to say, *"what the heck are those?"*
- I say *annuities* or *life insurance* and people run away!

How do you feel about these words?

Whatever you feel right now, please acknowledge that feeling with a bit of gratitude. It has served you well. But now set that feeling aside for a moment. It is my hope that you read the upcoming chapters with an open mind and an open heart. Remember that these securities and insurance products in the capital markets are just tools. They are not *good* tools or *evil* tools, despite what you may read about them or hear about them from well-known talking heads like Suze Orman or Dave Ramsey. Although both Suze and Dave offer a lot of great ideas on how to save and live debt free, they often share very biased opinions about the savings products offered in the capital markets due to the advertising revenue they get by becoming a biased voice toward one or more types of securities.

It is an unfortunate reality that many of these products can be misused by financial advisors and the clients they serve. But the blame on those misuses need to be directed at the advisor who is making the recommendation, not the security itself.

A hammer is just a tool. If I use it to build you a picnic table, it's a good tool. If I use it to whack your big toe, it's an evil tool. Or is it? It's really just a tool. I'm the good guy or the bad guy depending on what I do with that tool.

Regardless of your experience or what you may have read or heard before today, securities and insurance products like stocks, bonds, mutual funds, exchange traded funds, annuities and life insurance are all simply tools, just like the hammer. When used properly, every single one of these can have a meaningful impact on your ability to reach your financial goals. When used improperly or for the wrong reasons, each one of these can serve as a huge detriment to your financial independence.

The following chapters are designed to inform you of what's out there, how to use the products properly, and how to go about seeking advice and personalized guidance on how each of these might help you reach your most important financial objectives.

Whether your goal is to create a rainy day fund for emergencies, save a down payment for a first or second home, obtain enough assets to pay for college expenses, keep replacement income to handle an unexpected job loss, save for a secure retirement, or all of the above, proper use of these tools can be your keys to success.

Investing in Stock

Investing in stock has historically been one of the most effective ways to accumulate wealth for your financial future. If we are convinced that we must save money for tomorrow, stuffing our savings into a bank account with little ability to grow will hinder our ability to keep up with the rising cost of life.

If you were to put $20,000 into a low interest bank account today, ten years from now that same $20,000 would probably be worth less in terms of its purchasing power. What I mean by that is your $20,000 savings account of the future will likely buy you less in goods and services than it would today because of the long-term average of inflation at approximately 3 percent per year.

Not only does investing in stock provide you with the potential to maintain your purchasing power, it could also accelerate the growth of your savings beyond inflation and actually be worth *more* than what it buys you today.

The key to being successful in stock ownership is *time*. The sooner you start investing, the better chance you have of realizing the long-term return potential of stock ownership. However, if you are in a position where you are trying to rebuild your wealth as I did, then even a *late* start is better than *no* start!

A young family friend recently approached me about buying stocks. He wanted to invest $2,000 in a good stock or two to start his life-long journey of saving and investing. But he really didn't know what a stock was or how to go about buying it.

For new investors, buying stock does not have to be a difficult proposition. You should understand four basic things to get started:
- What stock is
- How to purchase stock
- A few simple ways to identify good stocks to own
- The basic rules of stock investing

What is stock?

Plain and simple, stock is a share in the ownership of a company. Stock represents a claim on the company's assets and earnings. As you acquire more stock, your ownership stake and influence within the organization become greater. Whether you say shares, equity, or stock, it all means the same thing. If you buy a company's stock, it technically means you own a tiny sliver of every part of the enterprise, from the furniture, to the trademark, and every client contract.

As an owner, you are entitled to your share of the company's earnings as well as any voting rights attached to the stock. For every share you own, normally you are entitled to one vote when it comes to electing the board of directors. The board oversees hiring and firing the key leadership, who in turn run the day-to-day decision-making and operations of the company. This vote happens every year at the annual shareholders' meeting.

Shareholders who do not attend this meeting (which is usually most shareholders) receive a voting proxy in the mail to cast their ballots, similar to the absentee ballots used in government elections. The more shares you own, the more influence you have over who makes the day-to-day decisions within the organization. For example, if you own one share of stock, you will have very little say about who gets elected to the board. But if you own 10 million shares, you may have substantial influence over who gets to run the company and how they choose to run it, especially if 10 million shares represent a large percentage of the total number of shares issued by the company. Heck, you might even find yourself with a seat on the board of directors!

How do I purchase shares of stock?

There are marketplaces around the world—much like grocery stores—that don't specialize in selling milk and bread. Instead, these markets, known as exchanges, buy and sell stock on behalf of investors. These exchanges are also referred to as the secondary market, because this is where existing (used) shares of stock are bought and sold.

Stock exchanges are run by specialists who know how to transact a purchase or a sale of stock shares between a buyer and a seller. These specialists earn a commission for helping someone buy or sell their shares on this exchange. Generally, these specialists work on behalf of a brokerage firm such as Charles Schwab. If you are a client of Charles Schwab, you would instruct your broker to buy or sell shares of stock on your behalf. Your broker would submit an electronic order for this "buy or sell" transaction to his trading desk. The trading desk would then work with an exchange specialist to execute the trade with another investor.

Brand new shares of stock can also be purchased, but only when a company issues new shares of stock through a process called a public offering. Basically, a company hires a big investment bank to analyze their balance sheet and tell them how much their company is worth. Then the bank breaks that total net worth up into shares and sells those shares to investors through an initial public offering (IPO).

The owners of privately-owned businesses will sometimes choose to convert their companies to publicly owned businesses to raise large sums of money. This cash is most commonly used to expand their business, buy other businesses, or to simply cash out and retire. In effect, these business owners trade a large portion of their ownership and control of their company for cash that they can use immediately as they see fit.

How do I identify good stocks to buy?

First, *be a loyal customer.*

Start your search with a small list of publicly-owned companies whose products or services you use and have been using for quite some time. Chances are you're not the only one who values what these companies do (or make).

What brand of coffee do you drink every day? What type of car do you drive? What type of smartphone or tablet do you own? These are good places to start narrowing your list of choices.

Second, *identify great leadership.* Once you narrow your list down to a handful of companies you spend your money with, learn everything you can about the leadership of those companies. The growth of an organization starts and ends with great leadership. Consider what you know about:

- Company culture
- Employee retention and experience
- Organizational operation
- Public image
- Customer service
- Mission

Finding out about these topics can come through simple Google searches and a bit of online reading. Simply search on "corporate culture of XYZ Company" and see what pops up. Determining whether a company has healthy growth in these areas is key to deciding if a company is worth investing your hard-earned dollars.

Third, *seek dividends.* A dividend is a profit distribution from a company to all its owners or shareholders. Companies generally pay dividends to their owners when they are healthy, stable, and highly profitable over a substantial period of time, and they want to use this dividend to share the success of the company with all shareholders.

Dividends can be paid in two ways: cash or stock. Cash dividends are paid directly to shareholders and can either be taken as cash or reinvested to buy more shares. Stock dividends are paid out in the form of additional shares of stock, usually in fractional amounts.

Following are two examples.

Let's say you own one hundred shares of ABC Company. ABC Company has announced they are paying shareholders an annual dividend of $.85 per share. For your one hundred shares, you will receive a check for $85 each year until the dividend amount changes. You can also choose to use your $85 to purchase more shares at whatever the current market price is for the stock. This is a simple example of a cash dividend.

Or perhaps ABC Company's board of directors declares they will issue a dividend in the form of .3 shares per share owned. That means, based on your 100 shares, you will receive thirty additional shares of ABC stock instead of a cash payout.

Companies will sometimes make stock dividend distributions rather than cash dividends if much of their cash is tied up in business-expanding investments and not available for dividend payments. Either way, paying regular, growing dividends in the form of cash or stock are a sign of a healthy organization.

BASIC RULES FOR STOCK OWNERS

Once you have found the right stock, you must follow the four rules of stock ownership.

1. Never buy a stock that you would ever have a reason to sell. What I mean by this is you must feel completely aligned with all aspects of the organization, from leadership to products to balance sheet. If a company makes a great product that is selling like wildfire, yet they have a heretic at the helm as CEO, at some point that lack of strong leadership could come back to hurt the company (possibly when the product falls out of favor).

2. Be patient. Stock prices do not necessarily grow in a straight line overnight. It's like planting a seed in a garden; it takes time and patience for that seed to become a delicious fruit. And obviously there are no guarantees—as with any market-based investment, you could lose money, too.

3. Buy a few more shares every month no matter what. The key to long-term investing with stocks is to gradually accumulate shares over your entire career of investing. Several chapters ago, we discussed the benefits of dollar-cost averaging, or making systematic monthly investments with the same dollar amount. By accumulating shares of a company over time, you are employing a strategy that—while not guaranteed to produce investment success or prevent losses—is nonetheless designed to help reduce your risk and lower the average price you pay per share.

4. Never mix your emotions with stock ownership. This one is pretty self-explanatory. The decision to own a fraction of a company is a business decision. There is nothing more dangerous than allowing emotions to dictate a business decision.

If you really love a certain company because their product is an important part of your life, the leadership is doing the right thing, and they pay dividends to their owners, chances are you may have found the right choice. Remember, as a stock owner, you are making a commitment to own part of this company for a long time. Your shares will fluctuate in value, sometimes going up and down for no apparent reason whatsoever. Check your emotions at the door and be prepared to buy more. And if you can't leave your emotions out of the mix, consider hiring a financial advisor who specializes in purchasing individual stocks.

This advisor can also be especially helpful when it's time to consider selling your ownership in these companies. Like all business owners, there will come a time in your life when divesting yourself of your shares will be a necessary strategy to provide the kind of retirement you will likely want. Talk to your financial advisor about how to structure your exit strategy from corporate ownership.

Congratulations. You are one step closer to becoming an owner in some of the most amazing companies in the world!

Making Sense of Bonds

Many of my clients own bonds, and as the stock market becomes more volatile, more clients ask questions about owning bonds for a larger portion of their portfolio.

Interestingly, I have found most people I meet know little about bonds, and for the most part, what they know is not quite accurate.

A common belief people have when they think of bonds is that they're safer than stocks.

They can be. But they can also involve a different set of risks.

Let's go back to basics and dive under the hood of the bond as an investment. Bonds are quite different than stocks. While a stock is a unit of ownership in a corporation, a bond is a form of debt. Typically, bonds are issued by companies, cities, schools, and governments as loans, or IOUs. The difference is you, the investor, serve as the bank. You loan them your money and they promise to pay you back in full at a certain date in the future through regular interest payments.

A company may sell bonds to purchase new computers or build a new facility. A school may sell bonds to build a new gymnasium. A city may sell bonds to build a new park. A state may sell bonds to repair highways. The federal government issues bonds to finance its increasing debt load.

Bonds tend to attract more conservative investors because of the steady stream of interest income they earn, as well as stock investors who flock to the perceived protection of bonds when the stock market becomes too volatile. However, despite the regular income payments investors receive through bonds, bonds are not risk-free. Some bonds can even carry more risk than stocks.

Risk in owning bonds is not always well understood by many investors. Risk comes in a few different varieties: credit risk, interest rate risk, call risk, reinvestment risk, and inflation risk.

Credit Risk

What is the likelihood the bond issuer will make good on its obligation to pay you back upon the stated maturity of the bond, as well as make interest payments each quarter or month?

Less credit-worthy issuers will pay a higher yield, or interest rate. That's why the riskiest issuers offer what's called high-yield, or "junk" bonds. They must pay you a higher interest rate to offset the higher risk that they may default on their loan to you. Those at the opposite end of the spectrum, with the best histories of repaying debts, are deemed investment-grade bonds, and generally pay a lower interest rate because you will likely not need to worry about a default.

The more conservative bonds from the standpoint of credit risk are those issued by the U.S. government, known as Treasurys. These bonds are backed by the "full faith and credit" of the federal government and are deemed virtually risk-free. The government has the ability to raise taxes and/or issue new debt to pay their existing debts, something most entities do not have the power to do. As such, a Treasury bond will pay a lower yield than a bond issued by a corporation or a school district.

Interest-Rate Risk

The longer the bond, the higher the interest rate you're paid. Bonds that mature in thirty years tend to pay more interest than bonds that mature in five years. You're being paid more for keeping your money tied up for a longer period of time. However, it's important to know that owning a longer bond (twenty or thirty years) exposes you to greater interest-rate risk.

Interest rates have the single largest impact on daily bond prices. As interest rates rise, bond prices fall. When rates climb, new bonds are issued at the higher rate, making existing bonds with lower rates less valuable in the current marketplace. The good news is that if you hold on to your bond until maturity, it doesn't matter how much the price fluctuates because the bond issuer agreed to pay you back the full-face amount (amount you invested originally) of the bond when it matures. But if you need to sell your bond on the secondary market before it matures, you could get less than your original investment back if interest rates rise and your bond becomes less valuable. The farther away your bond is from maturing, the more sensitive its price will be if interest rates fluctuate.

CALL RISK

Some bonds have a built-in safety feature for bond issuers, referred to as "call protection," that gives them the ability to "call" their bond away from you and return your money. If interest rates drop, this call feature allows issuers to basically erase their current debt and reissue new bonds at a lower interest rate. It's like having the option to refinance your debt.

The reason this poses a risk to investors is that many bond holders base a substantial portion of their retirement income on the interest they receive from their bond holdings. If a retiree has a large bond position called away, and must now buy lower-paying bonds, it could have a significant effect on the amount of income the retiree receives.

REINVESTMENT RISK AND INFLATION RISK

Like call risk, reinvestment risk can hurt bond investors if interest rates drop dramatically. Back in 1981, when then-Federal Reserve Chairman Paul Volcker was battling to contain hyperinflation, thirty-year bond yields topped 15 percent. Twenty-seven years later, during the crisis of 2008, the thirty-year yield plummeted to an all-time low of 2.55 percent.

Imagine if you had $1 million invested in thirty-year bonds in 1981. You would have been earning nearly $150,000 each year in interest payments. Those bonds would have matured in 2011, and if you were to renew them, your interest payment would drop to $25,500. Not only would your income have dropped substantially, but so would the amount of purchasing power your $1 million had.

In 1981, a postage stamp cost 18 cents. By 2011, a stamp cost increased by more than double to 44 cents. Your million-dollar bond investment today is worth about half of what it was worth in 1981, meaning it will buy you about half of what it could have bought you thirty years ago.

Now that we have reviewed the risks of owning bonds, let's briefly discuss the different types of bonds you can invest in and some of the common terminology associated with bond ownership.

As discussed earlier, *Treasurys* are issued by the U.S. government and are thus considered the most protected bonds on the market. As such, you won't collect as much in interest as you might elsewhere, but you don't have to worry about defaults. They're also used as a benchmark to price all other bonds, such as those issued by companies and municipalities.

Treasurys are available in $1,000 increments and are initially sold via auction, where the price of the bond and how much interest it pays out is determined. You can bid directly through TreasuryDirect.gov (with no fees) or through your bank or broker. They also trade like any regular security on the open market.

Treasury Bills, or *T-bills*, are a short-term investment sold in terms ranging from a few days to twenty-six weeks. They're sold at a discount to their face value ($1,000); however, when T-bills mature, you redeem the full-face value. You pocket the difference between the amount you paid and the face value, which is the interest you earned.

Treasury Notes are issued in terms of two, five and ten years, and in increments of $1,000. Mortgage rates are priced off of the ten-year note (more commonly called the ten-year bond, even though it's technically a note).

Treasury Bonds are issued in terms of thirty years. They pay interest every six months until they mature.

Treasury Inflation-Protected Securities (TIPS) are used to help protect your portfolio against inflation. TIPS usually pay a lower interest rate than other Treasurys, but their principal and interest payments, paid every six months, adjust with inflation as measured by the Consumer Price Index (CPI). It's often desirable to hold these in a tax-deferred account such as an IRA because you'll otherwise have to pay federal taxes on the increase in your bond value, even though you don't get the principal back until maturity. When TIPS do mature, investors receive either the adjusted principal or the original principal, whichever is greater. TIPS have five, ten, and twenty-year terms.

Savings Bonds are probably some of the most boring gifts out there, but it can't hurt to understand how they work. You can redeem your savings bonds after one year, and within up to thirty years. They're currently offered in two flavors, both issued by the U.S. Treasury: EE savings bonds and I savings bonds.

EE Savings Bonds earn a fixed rate of interest (currently 3.4 percent as of the writing of this book) and can be redeemed after one year (though you lose three months' interest if you hold them less than five years) but can be held for up to thirty years. When you redeem the bond, you'll collect the interest accrued plus the amount you paid for the bond. They can be purchased in the form of a paper certificate at a bank for half of their face value (for example, a $100 bond can be purchased for $50) in varying increments from $50 to $10,000. If they're purchased online, they're purchased at face value, but can be bought for any amount starting at $25.

I Savings Bonds are similar to EE savings bonds, except they're indexed for inflation every six months. These are always sold at face value, regardless of whether you buy paper or electronic versions.

Agency bonds are not quite as strong as Treasurys, yet they are often a better bet than the most pristine corporate bonds. They're issued by government-sponsored enterprises, like Fannie Mae and Freddie Mac (mortgage-backed bonds) and Sallie Mae (student-loan-backed bonds). Because these companies are chartered and regulated in part by the government, the bonds they issue are perceived to be more conservative than corporate bonds. They are not, however, backed by the "full faith and credit" of the U.S. government like Treasurys, which would make them virtually risk-free.

Municipal bonds, or *munis*, are issued by states, cities, and local governments to fund various projects. Municipals aren't subject to federal taxes, and if you live where the bonds are issued, they may also be exempt from state taxes. Some municipal bonds are more creditworthy than others, though some munis are insured. In this case, if the issuer defaults, the insurance company will have to cover the tab.

Corporate bonds are bonds issued by companies. Corporate debt can range from solid investments to super risky.

Coupon is another word for the interest rate paid by a bond. For instance, a $1,000 bond with a 6 percent coupon will pay $60 a year. The word coupon originates from when bonds actually had a paper coupon attached to them that could be redeemed for the payment, especially prior to 1990.

Par is also known as the face value of a bond, and is the amount a bondholder receives when the bond matures. If interest rates rise higher than the existing bond's rate, the bond will trade at a discount, or below par; if rates fall below the bond's rate, it will trade at a premium, or above par.

Duration is a measure of a bond price's sensitivity to a change in interest rates, measured in years. Bonds with longer durations are more sensitive to interest rate changes. If you're in a bond with a duration of ten years and rates rise 1 percent, the price of your bond will decline by 10 percent.

These are some of the great unknowns to many investors who think bond buying is super "safe." It is in this type of low-interest-rate environment that bond investors can really be caught off guard. If rates begin to rise and bond investors are forced to sell their bonds prior to maturity, they can be handed significant losses due to the rising rate environment. This can be even worse for investors who own their bonds inside bond mutual funds. When owning bond mutual funds, you no longer have the option of holding your bonds to maturity. A high-duration bond mutual fund could experience complete freefall in a sharply rising interest rate environment.

Maturity is the date your bond matures, and you receive all your principal back. Some bonds may get called away before their maturity date, but either way, you receive your par value back.

Like all possible investment tools, bonds may have a place inside a portfolio to provide everything from current income to appreciation potential. However, use caution when purchasing bonds. If you're a novice investor, I recommend you not go at it alone. Bond yields have been falling for nearly thirty years, which means prices have been rising. Many experts believe the bond market will be the next bubble to pop when rates begin to rise. Given that the bond market is considerably larger than the stock market, a bond bubble pop would be felt hard.

If you need some guidance purchasing bonds, I recommend working with a financial advisor in your community. Here are some resources to help you find someone with the requisite knowledge base:
- Certified Financial Planner Board of Standards
- Wiser Advisor.com
- The Financial Industry Regulatory Advisory's Broker Check

Mutual Funds vs. Exchange-Traded Funds (ETFs)

Exchange-traded funds (ETFs) are a big topic at Gebhardt Group, Inc. Clients and friends ask us quite often to help them better understand what these really are. I am amazed at how many people ask about them, because so many of them already own ETFs inside their retirement funds, whether they realize it or not.

ETFs have been around since the early 1990s, but really did not become popular in retirement plans until about ten years ago. Although ETFs have begun to gain popularity, the ETF market still pales in comparison to the mutual fund market, with about $1.7 trillion in ETFs versus $6.7 trillion in U.S. equity mutual funds, according to Morningstar.[6]

Ultimately, ETFs are the evolution of actively managed mutual funds and passively managed index funds. To truly understand the purpose and usefulness of this financial product, it's important to first understand its forerunners.

ACTIVELY-MANAGED MUTUAL FUNDS

A mutual fund is a big basket of individual investments like stocks (such as IBM, Proctor & Gamble, Apple, Coca-Cola, etc.). Every day, the fund issues new shares to those who want to own a "slice." It is the simplest way for investors to diversify their money with a small

---

[6] Taylor Tepper. Bankrate. January 9, 2019. "Mutual fund vs. ETF: Which is better?" https://www.bankrate.com/investing/mutual-fund-vs-etf-which-is-better/

investment amount: most fund companies let you purchase shares for as little as $2,000.

The best way to understand this structure and its benefits is to think of an extra-large pizza pie with a handful of toppings: pepperoni, sausage, olives, mushrooms, onions, and peppers (sort of makes you hungry, right?). You cut the pizza into eight slices and share it with a few friends. Each slice has a sampling of all the selected toppings on it. The best part of having multiple toppings is that if one is bad—say, the olives—people can just pick them off without ruining the whole slice.

Mutual funds work much the same way. If you invested all your retirement money in one individual stock, and that stock became worthless, you would be in big trouble. But if you invested your retirement money inside of a mutual fund, where you had a "slice" that contained samplings, or fractional shares of hundreds of stocks, you would be much less concerned if one went bad.

So, who manages mutual funds, and what are their goals?

Mutual funds rely on a portfolio manager, or a team of portfolio managers, to actively manage investments on behalf of others—for a fee. According to Morningstar, the average annual fee charged for a mutual fund is 0.48 percent.[7] This is also called an expense ratio. In addition to the expense ratio, a mutual fund can cost as much as 3.17 percent more per year in transaction fees, which are the costs portfolio managers incur for buying and selling stocks inside their funds. These costs can be more difficult to determine on a fund-by-fund basis because fund companies are not required to publish these additional expenses in their fund prospectus.[8]

To justify charging upward of 2.5 percent to 4 percent per year in total fees, portfolio managers hope their active management can take

---

[7] Ben Johnson. Morningstar. April 30, 2019. "Fund-Fee Study: The Key Factors Helping Drive Fund Fees Lower."
https://www.morningstar.com/blog/2019/04/30/us-fund-fee-study.html

[8] Roger Edelen. UC Davis. "Shedding Light on 'Invisible' Costs: Trading Costs and Mutual Fund Performance."
https://gsm.ucdavis.edu/sites/main/files/file-attachments/edelen_sheddinglighttradingcosts.pdf.

advantage of mispriced stocks or trends in the market to beat the overall market return. Unfortunately for most portfolio managers and their fund investors, history has proven that hope is not a successful strategy, as the majority of fund managers have failed to outperform their benchmarks, especially in the most recent decade.[9]

PASSIVELY-MANAGED INDEX MUTUAL FUNDS

Imagine the pizza we used to describe an actively managed mutual fund. Now, instead of a handful of toppings on it, imagine every topping ever created: 500, to be exact. Each slice would have a small sampling of 500 different toppings. I know what you're thinking: it would almost be impossible to distinguish the taste of one topping from another. But that was the strategy of John Bogle, founder of Vanguard Funds, who launched the first index mutual fund in 1976.

Bogle believed it was nearly impossible for any manager to beat the markets by actively trading a handful of stocks. He also believed it was in an investor's best interest to stay fully invested in the entire market at all times, riding it up and down for a long period.

Bogle's first index fund tracked the Standard and Poor's 500 Index (S&P 500). The fund was called the Vanguard 500. By owning all 500 stocks of the S&P 500, Bogle was able to offer a fund designed to keep up with the broad index of stocks. Since his fund was not actively managed, it cost very little to operate, which translated to a low cost for investors.

Wall Street and the financial advisory community were not fans of Bogle and his invention. They quickly slandered the Vanguard 500 Fund by referring to it as "Bogle's Folly." It was the belief of Wall Street and most financial advisors that their primary job was to beat the broad market and that Bogle's invention was a joke. Unfortunately, the joke was on Wall Street and the financial advisors. Few actually were

---

[9] Bob Pisani. CNBC. March 15, 2019. "Active fund managers trail the S&P 500 for the ninth year in a row in triumph for indexing."
https://www.cnbc.com/2019/03/15/active-fund-managers-trail-the-sp-500-for-the-ninth-year-in-a-row-in-triumph-for-indexing.html

able to beat their benchmarks and Bogle's Vanguard 500 Fund, especially once they added in their 2.5 to 3 percent each year in fees.[10]

Index funds have gained in popularity over the past three decades. Today there are hundreds of index funds, each tracking their own benchmark and typically at a fraction of the cost of actively managed mutual funds. They are some of the most popular fund offerings inside company-sponsored retirement plans.

WHAT IS AN ETF?

An ETF is a type of index fund. Like any index fund, it aims to provide investors with a low-cost product that offers the potential for broad market returns. There are, however, a couple of important differences.

First, index funds are like traditional mutual funds in that they are only priced once per day, at the close of the market session. The average price of all the underlying securities is calculated after the market closes, and the fund company posts the net asset value per share (NAV) based on the aggregate of all those prices. In contrast, ETFs are a fixed basket of securities that trade all day on the stock market, with the basket itself behaving more like an individual stock. The price of that basket of stocks can fluctuate all day based on the underlying values of the holdings within the ETF. This can give investors much greater liquidity, which gives them the ability to buy or sell shares quickly and at any time the market is open, rather than relying on a mutual fund or index fund that only prices itself once per day after the market closes.

The second main difference is the cost of trading mutual funds and index funds, compared to the cost of trading an ETF. Mutual funds and index funds often have significant transaction fees associated with buying or selling shares. Although most ETFs also incur transaction fees, some trade commission-free.

---

[10] Rob Berger. DoughRoller. May 15, 2019. "DR 063: The Four Hidden Fees of Mutual Funds."
https://www.doughroller.net/investing/the-four-hidden-fees-of-mutual-funds/

ETFs Version 2.0

As ETFs have grown in popularity, they are increasingly designed to do more than just mimic an index fund. Sector-specific ETFs, where all the holdings are from one specific sector (like healthcare or technology), have become quite popular. Many fee-only financial advisors have adopted ETFs into their practices as efficient tools to actively manage client portfolios and gain exposure to multiple sectors of the market.

But "do-it-yourselfers," beware. There are risks and complexities associated with buying and selling ETFs. If you are a DIY investor and you want to have the flexibility of an ETF's low trading cost and performance similar to an index fund, you may want to use only the largest, most widely traded ETFs—the ones designed to match well-known benchmarks. The smaller sector-based ETFs often have much less liquidity on a daily basis, as fewer shares are traded compared to the big index-based ETFs. Also, like mutual funds, ETF performance can vary widely from issuer to issuer—even those that seem to track the same benchmark or sector.

ETFs have become the next great innovation in the mutual and index fund universe. They can be efficient investment products and are showing their rise in popularity by popping up more and more inside company-sponsored retirement plans.

If you own a retirement account and you choose to go at it alone selecting your ETFs, please do your homework. Managing an active portfolio of ETFs is not for novice investors with a weekend hobby. Work with a professional whenever possible.

Is an Annuity Right for Me?

One of the most viciously targeted and often scrutinized financial tools in existence is the deferred annuity. Various factions on Wall Street, in the media, and even in government and politics seem to have made it their mission to discredit the deferred annuity as a viable option for a portion of one's retirement savings. They often cite high fees, illiquidity, and product complexity as the primary reasons the "wretched" deferred annuity is the average investor's arch-nemesis.

I have a problem with this generalization of a financial tool.

Is a hammer good or bad? I hope your answer is, "Depends on how it's used." If I use a hammer to rebuild a deck in your back yard, it's a good tool. If you stiff me on payment, and I use that hammer to destroy your new deck, the hammer is a bad tool.

The same can be said about deferred annuities. The deferred annuity is simply a tool—a rather complex one, to be sure—but a tool nonetheless. The key to making it work right is to apply it correctly to the right circumstance. Unfortunately, too many financial advisors do not fully understand the best applications for deferred annuities, and then sell them to clients when they are not appropriate vehicles. How can you blame the deferred annuity? It's not the hammer's fault if I hit you over the head with it.

Quit picking on the annuity, please, and let's place blame where I feel it belongs: on selfish or undereducated financial professionals whose only concern is making a hefty commission for themselves.

Let's take a step back and look at what an annuity actually is and where it may be appropriate for a portion of your retirement savings.

We'll start with a simple definition of the word "annuity." An annuity is an insurance contract that is synonymous with income. Over time or as a lump sum, the contract owner pays into the contract with the insurance company. When the contract owner is ready to receive an income stream, the money they have paid starts coming back to them as income, usually promised for life or a fixed period like ten, twenty, or thirty years. These two distinct phases of the annuity's life span are referred to as the **accumulation phase** (the time you pay into the annuity) and the **annuity phase** (the period of time the annuity pays you).

There are two main categories of annuities: immediate and deferred. Extrapolating our original definition of an annuity as income, one can easily conclude what the primary difference is between immediate and deferred annuities: an immediate annuity begins payments now. A deferred annuity begins payments later.

Let's take it a step further.

Within the immediate and deferred annuity camps, there are two sub-categories that define the type of accumulation (or growth potential) you receive during the first phase of ownership: fixed and variable. The difference between fixed and variable (as one might guess) is that fixed annuities grow and accumulate at a set, locked-in fixed percentage for the duration of the accumulation phase of the contract, and a variable annuity accumulates or grows at a variable rate that can change throughout the duration of the accumulation period of the contract.

Now that we've covered the basic terms, let's put a few of them together to show you how different annuities are designed.

Fixed lifetime immediate annuity: This kind of annuity provides income now and pays a fixed interest rate for life.

Deferred variable annuity: This is an annuity that creates income later in life by allowing you to defer that income at a variable rate, or a changing rate of return. Often that variable rate of return is delivered in the form of variable sub-accounts, which invest in underlying mutual funds, inside deferred variable annuities that you and your advisor choose with the hopes for a good return over time, and which ultimately provide you with income down the road. Variable annuities are market-based investments, so unlike all other annuities, it is possible to also lose money due to market downturns.

Fixed index deferred annuity: This is a much more complex structure that allows you to earn interest based on changes in an external index without ever being invested in the market. These products offer guarantees on your money and the ability to defer guaranteed lifetime income for the future. Many offer a fixed minimum income value (assuming you buy the rider that provides this benefit), and also allow you the potential to capture a portion of a stock or bond market index return via interest credits to boost that future income amount.

There are many more types of annuity products on the market today. When used properly for the right reasons, annuities can be one of the best investments you ever make, especially if your goal is to create guaranteed income to last your entire lifetime. And like all financial products, they involve fees and charges, including surrender charges for early withdrawals, so you need to understand how they work in order to decide if they make sense for you.

Let's face it: retirement is completely on our shoulders. That means it's up to us to figure out how to replace our career income with retirement income, once we get to the point in life where our "have-to's" get replaced by "want-to's." Foundational expenses in retirement like housing, food, and medical care must be covered by foundational income sources (pensions if you're one of the lucky ones, plus Social Security, bond interest, rental income, etc.). Should you find a gap between your estimated foundational expenses and foundational sources of income, an annuity can be an excellent tool to fill that space. Discretionary expenses such as travel, dining out, second homes, etc. can be based on the remainder of your retirement assets to create the discretionary income you need; those assets are typically exposed to more risk-based assets such as stocks, bonds, mutual funds, ETFs, and real estate.

Annuities can be complex tools, and they certainly require the assistance of a professional. This person must have much more than just excellent product knowledge. He or she must also intimately know the details of your life, so together you can determine if an annuity makes sense for you . . . and if so, what type. Trust is the key element, as you must trust this professional enough to open up and be completely transparent about your aspirations, your lifestyle, and how you see your vision of your ideal future. Anything less than that can cause a bad fit with an annuity product and contract holder, leading to a less-than-desired outcome.

Remember, a hammer is a great tool when used to build a deck, but it quickly becomes evil if it's used to destroy your deck against your wishes. Having a properly structured and funded annuity can mean the difference between a happy retirement traveling the world versus a stressful retirement filled with uncertainty and undesirable part-time jobs.

Deep down, many of us like the peace of mind that comes with owning a pension, but few of us have corporate pensions. Instead, we can look to annuities to offer similar streams of income throughout our lifetimes.

To Insure or Not to Insure

One of my favorite movie characters of all time is Ned Ryerson, a gregariously slick life insurance salesman played by actor Stephen Tobolowsky in the 1993 movie *Groundhog Day*. If you are not familiar with the movie or the story line, it's a comedy about a weatherman who finds himself inexplicably living the same day over and over again. It's ninety minutes of belly laugh after belly laugh, and I recommend you put it on your watch-very-soon list.

As a life insurance salesman, Ned is seen accosting the film's main character, Pittsburgh weatherman Phil Connors (played by Bill Murray), day-in and day-out as Connors is stuck reliving Groundhog's Day over and over. Ned is your stereotypical life insurance salesman. He doesn't care much about Phil; all he cares about is selling clients on his hottest new product: single premium life insurance.

Fictional film and television do a fantastic job of poking fun at the stereotypes associated with cheesy sales people. From life insurance to used cars, art has a way of imitating real life. However, far too many people allow these stereotypes to cloud good financial decision-making when it comes to things like buying life insurance.

In this chapter, we will look at the basic types of life insurance and where they might be used as powerful financial tools to offset some major financial risks throughout one's lifetime.

Life Insurance was initially created as a unique financial instrument to allow an individual to transfer a large unknown risk (i.e. premature death) to a big insurance company in exchange for a much smaller known risk (i.e. premium payments). If the main income earner in a household dies prematurely and does not have a plan in place like life insurance, that income earner leaves his or her family without the necessary income to pay bills and live life. That's a huge risk that effects nearly 900,000 families each year, according to the CDC.[11] Life insurance is a way to transfer that financial risk away from the family and onto the shoulders of a large life insurance company. Should that income earner die prematurely, the insurance company would provide the surviving family members a large sum of money to replace the lost income of the deceased. In exchange for taking on that financial obligation to your family, you, the income earner, are required to pay that insurance company each year for that protection; a fractional cost commonly referred to as a "premium."

Since the insurance company is potentially on the hook for a lot of money to any one family, the process for purchasing this kind of premature death protection includes underwriting to determine what you, the insured, should pay for this protection. The insurer will consider many aspects of your lifestyle for pricing, such as current medical record, driving record, and criminal record. It is important for the insurance company to assess your likelihood of premature death in determining the cost of your life insurance policy. For insurance companies to successfully protect millions of families from the financial burden of premature death, they must remain financially healthy. That means insurance companies must collect more money through premium payments than they pay out insurance claims to be able to guarantee their claims-paying ability to those 900,000 families each year who need it.

Like the annuities we discussed in the previous chapter, life insurance can be divided into two main categories: permanent (cash-value) life insurance, and term (temporary) life insurance. The main difference between the two is that permanent is designed to provide

---

[11] Centers for Disease Control and Prevention. May 1, 2014. "Up to 40 percent of annual deaths from each of five leading US causes are preventable." https://www.cdc.gov/media/releases/2014/p0501-preventable-deaths.html

protection for your entire lifetime, whereas term is designed to last for a specific period of time, say ten or twenty years.

Term insurance is the simplest and fastest way to protect your family against premature death of your family's primary income earners. It's relatively inexpensive to purchase, and the underwriting process is usually simple. Often, people who apply for $1,000,000 or less in life insurance coverage can complete the underwriting process by simply answering a few questions about their health. Sometimes an insurance company will require a doctor to provide health records or blood work if the applicant has any history of chronic or critical conditions such as heart disease, kidney disease or cancer. The lower your risk of premature death, the less expensive your insurance policy is. A non-smoker in excellent health, buying $1 million in term coverage for twenty years at the age of thirty could expect to pay as little as $50 to $75 per month for their policy.

The main drawback to term coverage is that when the term of coverage is over, your protection is gone, as are all of the premiums you paid for that protection. The thirty-year-old who purchased a $1 million policy that expired at age fifty could likely purchase a new policy assuming he or she is still in good health. However, at age fifty, the risk of death over the next twenty years is much greater, therefore creating a much greater cost of that same $1 million in coverage. That same policy issued at age fifty could cost as much as $500 per month. Over the course of forty years, term policies structured in this way would cost as much as $132,000 in total premiums for $1 million in premature death protection. That $132,000 is often money well spent, however it is gone after the policies reach their termination and there is no remaining value left to the policy holder.

This is where permanent life insurance, or cash-value life insurance, can become a lot more appealing. Although permanent insurance is often scoffed at for being more expensive than term insurance, the extra "cost" associated with permanent insurance accumulates inside of the policy as cash value for the benefit of the policy holder _while they are still alive_. What that means is all of the premiums paid into the policy do not disappear if the policy is not used to pay out a death claim. Instead, part of the premium is used to pay for the cost of the death benefit and any excess amount not needed to pay for the death benefit accumulates inside the policy as cash value to the policy holder. That growing cash value can be withdrawn from the policy at a later date, usually in the form of a tax-free loan that does not need to be paid back while you're still alive.[12] Upon death, the loan against your cash value is ultimately paid back using a portion of the death benefit. The remaining death benefit goes to your family.

I knew very little about how these permanent or cash value life insurance policies worked until we met a client who owned one of these policies and we saw how this all worked firsthand through their experience. Peter and Tammy, who were both in their fifties, came into our office in 2014 with an urgent need for financial planning—they were experiencing a challenging life transition. Tammy was a medical assistant working for an oral surgeon in town. Peter was a thirty-year employee of a local bank. He had accumulated a large 401(k) balance and had lots and lots of company stock. All in all, Peter and Tammy were worth just north of $3 million, the majority of which was in retirement accounts and deferred stock accounts. They also owned a permanent life insurance policy with a $2 million death benefit and terminal illness rider that gave them access to up to $500,000 of the death benefit, should they need it in Peter's lifetime.

Their transition was Peter's recent diagnosis of Amyotrophic Lateral Sclerosis (ALS), commonly known as Lou Gehrig's disease. This diagnosis meant Peter, Tammy, and their two daughters had to face the reality that Peter would not live beyond a few more years. It meant he would eventually lose all of his mobility and would have to leave his job and nice salary and try to survive on long-term disability

---

[12] Policy loans and withdrawals will reduce available cash values and death benefits, and may cause the policy to lapse or affect any guarantees against lapse. Additional premium payments may be required to keep the policy in force. In the event of a lapse, outstanding policy loans in excess of unrecovered cost basis will be subject to ordinary income tax. Tax laws are subject to change. You should consult a tax professional.

payments, which were less than half of what he and his family were accustomed to. With both girls in college and a sizable mortgage payment to make each month, this presented quite a financial challenge. It also meant Tammy and Peter would have to live their retirement dream of travel and experiencing the world now instead of when they originally intended. With Peter's income cut in half, this early retirement was nearly impossible to envision. They were scrambling just to figure out how to pay the bills during the last few years of Peter's life. It initially appeared as if they would be forced to take early distributions from Peter's retirement accounts.

The idea of paying income taxes plus a 10 percent early distribution penalty for using Peter's 401(k) to support themselves left both Peter and Tammy feeling insecure about her future once Peter was gone. This is where I began to learn about the benefits of having cash value life insurance. Instead of tapping Peter's 401(k), they were able to use the terminal illness rider (living benefits) of Peter's life insurance policy to help them pay bills, take a few trips, and ultimately redo their home to accommodate Peter's care needs as his ALS progressed. This allowed us to keep all of Peter's retirement assets intact while providing the financial relief they both so desperately needed.

Peter ultimately succumbed to his illness in February of 2018. After withdrawing enough money to cover their income needs for the final few years of Peter's life, his life insurance policy still paid out nearly $1.5 million, tax-free, for Tammy and her girls. They now have that financial resource to help them rebuild their lives free from the worry of how to make ends meet on a day-to-day basis. Peter's entire retirement savings remained intact so Tammy will not have to worry about running out of money during her lifetime. Without Peter's permanent life insurance policy, Tammy would have been left with the immense worry of unknowns about her future financial security, which would be on top of mourning the loss of her husband. Thankfully, because of their decision to purchase permanent insurance, Tammy's only job now is to hug her daughters and heal.

This Ain't Your Granddad's Life Insurance Anymore

Think back to your first mobile phone device. Mine was a small Motorola flip phone, and it did one thing really well: it made phone calls. Today, I own an elaborate device called a smartphone. Sure, it still makes phone calls. But it's also so much more. It's my calculator, my camera, my email device, my calorie counter, my dictionary, and my virtual assistant. The traditional phone has evolved into the Swiss Army knife of mobile computing. It does nearly everything I can think of where technology touches my life, leaps and bounds beyond what my first flip phone was able to do for me.

Life insurance has undergone the same kind of evolution. When I bought my first twenty-year term insurance policy in 1997 as a newlywed, it was designed to do one thing and only one thing: replace my income for my wife if I were to die prematurely. Today, life insurance has evolved into more of a Swiss Army knife, much like my smartphone. It is still there to protect my family against my premature death, but it can now do so much more. It can be my disability income if I were to get hurt or sick. It can be my long-term care insurance if I need custodial help one day. It can be a source of tax-free retirement income if I just happen to stay healthy and live a long time. In the end, anything I don't use will benefit my family once I'm gone.

There are many different types of temporary and permanent life insurance options. It is important to work with an expert to determine what is the right kind for you and how much you should own. You also need to carefully manage your policy's cash values, since withdrawing too much can deplete its value while you're alive—requiring additional premium payments to keep it in-force. It can get confusing and complicated and is a conversation that is easy to put off or ignore altogether. No one likes to discuss the awful circumstances that necessitate life insurance. But once you've witnessed the real-life experiences of people close to you, and how life insurance made all the difference, you become a fierce advocate of the need and urgency of having that conversation before it's too late.

Thirty-Year Plan
for a Retirement on Purpose

Retirement: (n) re-tire-mint: as defined by Gebhardt Group, Inc.: a major life transition point where one has achieved financial independence and a clear vision of purpose. Occupation becomes choice rather than necessity.

Planning for retirement is much more than saving money. It is a preparation process that requires time, dedication, discipline, and contemplation.

A few generations ago, retirement planning seemed simpler. One worked for thirty years, usually for the same organization, and by age sixty-five, reached the ceremonial finish line. Life expectancies once in retirement were about seven to ten years. A secure retirement was promised and provided through pensions, health care, and Social Security. Time was often spent in year-round sunshine playing tennis, golf, or bridge, and then meeting friends at Tony Roma's for the Early Bird dinner at 4:30 p.m. This period of life, once referred to as the "golden years" was golden because of its simplicity and comfort.

Today, just a few generations later, the landscape of retirement has completely changed. Some might argue it has changed for the worse, while some think it has changed for the better. With life expectancies reaching into the mid-to-late eighties, it's becoming common to see a retirement last twenty or more years. As more people even reach their nineties and hundreds, retirement can last as long as forty years. For many, that equates to more time spent in retirement than time invested in the working years preparing for retirement.

For those who plan properly, the twenty to forty years "after work" can have substantial meaning and purpose. It can allow one to feel incredibly fulfilled by having a massive impact on family and future generations, even more so than the time spent "working" the previous thirty years.

The path to proper retirement planning requires preparation in three areas:
- Financial preparedness
- Choice and control
- Purpose

FINANCIAL PREPAREDNESS

Paying for life in retirement is almost completely on our shoulders now. Pension benefits have virtually vanished in the private sector, and they have been significantly reduced in the public sector. Our Social Security and Medicare programs are running on fumes and their future is uncertain. Both were social welfare programs created after the Great Depression of the 1930s to keep the elderly (with short life expectancies) out of poverty. At the time, life expectancies were around sixty, and there were nearly 160 people working to support every one person receiving benefits.[13]

Now life expectancies are much longer, and because of the roughly 77 million baby boomers reaching retirement, the ratio of worker to retiree has been dramatically reduced to approximately three to one. Over the next decade or two, this ratio could be reduced to one worker for every one retiree. This will require radical changes in both Social Security and Medicare, if not the complete elimination of one or both as they exist today as a retirement benefit for everyone.[14] Many

---

[13] Social Security. "Social Security History: Frequently Asked Questions." https://www.ssa.gov/history/ratios.html
[14] Peter G. Peterson Foundation. April 23, 2019. "Five Charts About the Future of Social Security and Medicare."

politicians and business leaders support the idea of means-testing to qualify for benefits, in effect reverting back to the original reasons these programs were created: to keep retirees out of poverty.

Financial independence now requires a lifetime of financial preparation. For today's sixty-five-year-old to live comfortably on $100,000 per year for the rest of his or her life (assuming they no longer want to work), one would need approximately $2.5 million saved to minimize the risk of running out of money, if we exclude Social Security. For today's forty-year-old planning to retire in twenty-five years, that same $100,000 lifestyle today will need to be $200,000 in twenty-five years just to buy the same stuff (thank you, 3% long-term historical inflation!). That will require retirement savings of $5 million. This is certainly attainable, but it requires the discipline of long-term saving and avoiding the indulgences of overspending on meaningless stuff.

CHOICE AND CONTROL

Retirement can be a choice and it can happen on your terms, doing it when you want to, how you want to, and where you want to. Retirement is also something that needs to be completely redefined based your own personal meaning.

Years ago, retirement meant "nothingness:" a few rounds of golf, a gold watch, and then you were gone. Today, retirement could be the most significant period in one's life, especially if it happens on purpose (which is the way I recommend you do it). Planning for choice and control becomes a reality when we can define *why* we want to retire.

Steve Jobs is a great example of someone who retired young. Everything he did, especially in the latter half of his life, was about choice. Steve didn't have to work. He was financially prepared for retirement by his late thirties. Despite having enough money to sit on a beach, sipping margaritas for the rest of his life, Steve Jobs chose to

---

https://www.pgpf.org/blog/2019/04/five-charts-about-the-future-of-social-security-and-medicare

transform the way the world communicates. The effect of his purpose—his *why*—has been felt across civilization. Not only did he turn Apple into the most valuable company on the Earth, he transformed the definition of communication for nearly everyone in the developed world.

My parents, Henry and Jill Grishman, are also retired. Like Steve Jobs, they have chosen and maintained control over their retirement. My mother, Jill, was a school teacher who retired in 2010 to care for her parents and spend more time with her grandchildren. My father, Henry, has been retired for nearly fifteen years (based on my definition of retirement), yet at age seventy-four he still goes to his office almost every day at the Jericho Union Free School District in central Nassau County, New York.

Henry has been a school superintendent since 1977 and is currently one of the longest-serving superintendents in the country. He is the best at his craft, and he loves his job each and every day. Henry is clear on his why, and as a result, he has had a direct impact on shaping the lives of thousands of children over a four-decade career. My parents have been such incredible role models for me in defining retirement and what is necessary to be in a position of choice and control by age fifty-five.

Not bad for a couple of school teachers! It is their example that I use most to guide clients in defining their why and preserving as much choice and control over their own retirement.

Despite Steve Jobs' and my parents' ability to choose and control their retirement, there are certainly factors outside of any person's control that can force someone to consider retirement before they are financially ready. However, long-term preparation and attentiveness to one's true unique abilities can minimize the burden these unforeseen circumstances can place on a forced decision to retire. This is the most critical planning piece that should be well-defined if having control and choice are to become a reality. The key element to this planning is attaching financial preparedness to finding purpose.

Purpose

Many retirees, as well as people in their thirties, forties, and fifties working toward retirement, struggle with the emotional and social changes of transitioning into retirement. Retirement is no longer about "nothingness." It's a stage of life that might last longer than one's working years. Therefore, investing the proper time to reflect on "what's next" is a critical part of the retirement planning process.

Is "next" a second career? Is it writing a book, volunteering, or going back to school? Is it traveling the world, or learning how to fly a plane, or building furniture? The key to answering these big questions is to sit quietly and listen carefully to what your soul tells you. It's not a thinking process; it's a feeling process.

In our wealth management practice, we help clients begin the inner dialogue about what's next by helping them define their true wealth. We do this by taking families through a proprietary process called the GGI Wealth F.O.R.M.ation Experience™. Our process allows clients to measure their true wealth in four major categories: Family, Occupation, Recreation, and Money. The Family category is about defining the most important people in a person's life and becoming acutely aware of the impact they have on one's happiness. We'll come back to Occupation, as that is the key part of the purpose work that needs to happen prior to retirement. Recreation is the category that defines the fun in life: what a person enjoys doing most with the people he or she cares about most. Money is the category where we identify and document one's belief system about money and how money serves the most important aspirations one has in life. We also establish the steps necessary to accumulate and protect the amount of money identified to support one's true wealth.

Occupation is the category of true wealth that is often simpler to define in the working years of life. Occupation is about how people outwardly share their unique abilities for the benefit of their family, their community, and the entire world. Occupation is expressed in a variety of ways: working, volunteering, and coaching youth sports, to name a few examples. Occupation is a key ingredient in one's overall happiness and fulfillment in life. As one approaches retirement, Occupation can become more difficult to define. People are often challenged to figure out what's next as they transition from "have to" mode to "want to" mode.

Do you know what your new occupation will be in retirement?

Purpose work becomes an important component to the retirement planning process, as it ties the three parts of planning into one holistic definition of retirement. This can often take years of hard work and self-examination. With proper planning and coaching, one's true purpose will show up and the pieces of retirement will fall into place.

When people are clear on who they are, what they're supposed to do, and, critically, why they're supposed to do it, choice, control, financial preparation, and purpose come together to create a dynamic plan for happiness, gratification, and significance in retirement.

This is no small task. The biggest mistake made in the retirement planning years is developing a belief that retirement planning is simply about saving money. That could not be further from the truth. Putting all three pieces in place happens at different points in life, with some definite overlap.

Creating the Thirty-Year Plan for a Retirement on Purpose looks like this:

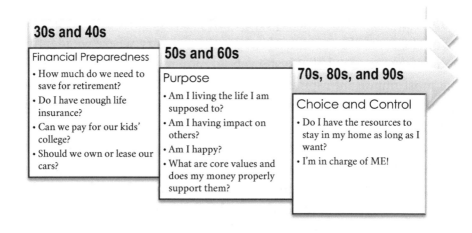

Financial planning and preparation generally begin at around thirty years old. If done correctly and consistently, this should take approximately twenty-five years to complete. Purpose work usually begins around forty. For some clients, finding a well-defined purpose for retirement can happen quickly, sometimes as soon as five years or less. For most, purpose work is a ten- to twenty-year process of clearly defining one's unique abilities and exploring how those abilities can be applied to 80 percent or more of the time spent in Occupation. It's important to first establish your financial preparedness, and then you are able to be clear on your purpose and choice. Only then can you have control and clarity over the journalist's questions of retirement: When, why, how, who, and what.

There is great satisfaction in this moment of retirement "on purpose." For many, it is the greatest victory in life. It is most common to experience it somewhere between fifty-five and sixty-five years old; however, it can happen sooner. It happened for me at thirty-eight.

This moment can create a feeling of satisfaction and self-fulfillment that extends way beyond any previous accomplishment, including marriage and raising kids. This definition of retirement is available to anyone who chooses consciously to build a Thirty-Year Plan.

Retirement is no longer provided to us. We must choose to create our golden years. It takes planning, dedication, discipline, persistence, and time. It also takes a real pro by your side to guide you, a wealth coach to help you stay accountable to enjoying the journey and achieving the ultimate success in life: a retirement on purpose.

Guiding others on this journey has become my occupation. And I do it on purpose.

The Multi-Phase Retirement

There are many definitions of retirement circulating through dictionaries across the globe that you can easily find with the click of a mouse. Wikipedia defines retirement as "the point where a person stops employment completely. A person may also semi-retire by reducing work hours."[15] Merriam-Webster defines it as "the act of ending your working or professional career; the act of retiring; the state of being retired; the period after you have permanently stopped your job or profession."[16]

You read my definition of retirement in the last chapter, which is "a major life transition point where one has achieved financial independence and a clear vision of purpose. Occupation becomes choice rather than necessity."

Is retirement a homogeneous period of time in one's life that is simply defined by not working anymore? If that's the case, then planning should be pretty simple, right? All we need to do is calculate how much money we need to save to provide for life after work and all will be okay, right?

Wrong!

In fact, the definitions I found online could not be farther from the truth of what retirement really is. Society as a whole has failed both the baby boomers and Generation X by selling retirement (and the

---

[15] Wikipedia. "Retirement."
https://www.wikipedia.com/retirement
[16] Merriam-Webster. "Retirement."
https://www.merriam-webster.com/dictionary/retirement

process of planning for it) as a simple money issue—accumulating money and distributing money (a fancy way of saying saving and spending). Financial advice has been driven by a belief that basic asset allocation (a fancy term for "spreading your money out over several kinds of investments") with your retirement savings will accumulate over time (saving) and provide you with modest distributions (spending) for your entire life. Television commercials depict this dream daily: retired couples strolling on the beach, or playing golf, or traveling with friends, followed by a celebrity voice describing promises of investment and insurance strategies to help you pay for these golden moments of recreation. But defining and planning your retirement is much more than how to pay for your travel.

Over the past twenty years, I've seen people of all ages struggle with the emotional side of retirement as well as the transition through the different tiers of retirement. With a little discipline and a winning strategy, the savings side of retirement planning is pretty simple. On the other hand, there are some not-so-simple parts to the retirement puzzle the financial planning industry is failing to help people with:

- Figuring out what you're going to do for the rest of your life.
- The right timing of your retirement.
- Managing the different phases of a multi-decade retirement.

As I discussed in the previous chapter, people are living longer. Retirement is often a twenty-, thirty-, or even forty-year proposition. It is now possible to experience a retirement that lasts longer than the pre-retirement years of working and saving for it. Planning for retirement requires a much deeper strategy besides a good target series fund in your retirement, followed by a rollover to an IRA and a 4 percent withdrawal rate.

We teach our clients that retirement is comprised of three distinct phases that all have a different effect on your savings and your emotional well-being. We call them:

- The Go-Go Phase
- The Slow-Go Phase
- The No-Go Phase

Each phase requires proper planning, as our lifestyles change dramatically from one phase to the next. There's no set formula that dictates how long each phase lasts, and the transitions between them are sometimes not well defined. Proper planning is paramount so that when a transition does occur, you are ready and prepared. I realize that the following explanations of these three phases are somewhat simplistic and rather broad. Each person we meet experiences some commonality with all other retirees, but also has unique needs and transition timelines from one phase to the next. These portrayals of the three phases of retirement are based on twenty years of observations from my partner and me in our private practice and within our own families.

THE GO-GO PHASE

The Go-Go Phase is the time often defined by freedom, constant activity, and recreation. Traveling to see the grandkids, visiting the bucket list destinations, and dining out with friends are all signature experiences of the Go-Go Phase of retirement. Work can still be a big part of the Go-Go Phase, but now all work happens out of choice rather than obligation. Assuming people have uncovered their true unique abilities and found a way to give them to the world, they can spend a significant portion of their lives in this "doing" space.

Although living expenses can be high in the Go-Go Phase, typically these costs do not come with significant inflation. Travel, food, and entertainment have not seen a great deal of inflation the past few decades, so planning for this phase is quite different than the latter phases of retirement, where inflation is moving at hyper-speed. The assets you set aside for the Go-Go Phase can be conservatively positioned, with growth that keeps up with or slightly exceeds core inflation (1 to 2 percent). Generally, we see our clients incur an asset burn rate (withdrawals from retirement savings) close to or even slightly greater than their living expenses prior to retirement.

One of the key components to a solid multi-phase retirement plan is to set aside a full year's worth of cash to finance an entire year of living expenses. The common practice implemented by your average run-of-the-mill brokerage firm is to take monthly distributions from your retirement savings to cover your expenses. It is my belief, based on working with Go-Go retirees, that this is a flawed strategy; it puts too much pressure on retirement savings to perform beyond the desired withdrawal rate each and every year.

Let's look at this a bit closer.

The average withdrawal rate recommended by Wall Street brokers and mutual fund companies is generally 3 to 4 percent annually (broken into monthly or quarterly distributions).[17] They claim that if you maintain these modest withdrawal rates, you have a low probability of outliving your assets. But that doesn't tell the whole story. During the decade of 2000 to 2010, the first official decade of massive baby boomer retirements, the market barely squeaked out a 4 percent annual average return. Add to that paltry return the annual expenses of the mutual funds your broker would have you in, and you were likely barely in the positive.

In the past two years, I have met many retirees who came to me after retiring in the mid-2000s with less than half of what they started with at retirement. Why? In a decade of horrendous returns, the portfolio was pressured to produce current income through monthly withdrawals. It's simply more proof of yet one more outdated belief that often benefits the brokerage firms and mutual fund companies more than the retirees they're supposed to be serving.

As fiduciaries devoted to serving the best interest of our clients, we implement a strategy that sets aside an entire year's worth of cash at the beginning of every calendar year, allowing a client (especially those newly retired and in the Go-Go Phase) to access what they need to live on and allow the remainder of their portfolio to work without the stress of producing current income.

---

[17] Dana Anspach. November 11, 2018. "How the 4 Percent Rule Works in Retirement."
https://www.thebalance.com/what-is-the-4percent-rule-in-retirement-2388273

THE SLOW-GO PHASE

We have observed that most of our clients enter the second phase of retirement somewhere between five to fifteen years after retirement officially begins. Physically, they are often still in good shape. They have reached a point in life where they have "been there, done that" and enjoy staying closer to home. They invite the children to come visit. They cook more than they dine out, and they really get connected to their home and a small community of inner circle relationships. Couples often remodel their home to reflect how they want to use it at this point in their lives. Cost of living tends to decline a bit, as they do not spend as much on travel and leisure. However, a home renovation in the Slow-Go Phase could weigh heavily on one's assets, so careful planning is necessary.

Planning for the Slow-Go Phase requires a look into the things in life one truly enjoys ... the simple things. Long walks, Sunday drives, watching the grandchildren play Little League baseball, a favorite movie, cooking a favorite dish. The Slow-Go Phase also comes with great contemplation. It is a time in one's life where people decide if they have truly lived their life's purpose. They sit back and enjoy seeing their legacy in their children and grandchildren. Financially, they can take their foot off the gas pedal as their spending generally slows. This phase can have the least demand on assets, so setting aside a portion that modestly grows beyond inflation is wise.

When planning for this phase, we set aside a portion of client assets that we intend to invest for a little longer period of time. Clients generally do not need access to this money for five to fifteen years. Therefore, we tend to focus on tax-efficient growth strategies to maximize the growth potential so that these assets can do their job and pay for those living expenses incurred throughout the Slow-Go Phase.

THE NO-GO PHASE

The last phase in retirement is one that can last ten or more years. One of the realities of life is that, at some point, our bodies will age and not function as they used to. We may spend most of our time at home and/or visiting doctors. We will need more medical care and possibly help around the house with everyday tasks like cooking, cleaning, bathing, and driving.

This can also become the most expensive phase of retirement. Financial preparation for this phase requires some complex planning separate from the planning required for the first two phases. Your savings must grow at a much greater rate than core inflation, as prices of health care and home care are accelerating at a rate much higher than core inflation. Despite inflation decreasing in health care since the enactment of the Affordable Care Act, health care costs still grow at a rate that is nearly double that of core inflation.[18]

Once the financial preparation is complete, the more difficult task of preparing for the emotional transition between the Slow-Go Phase and No-Go Phase must begin. This is no easy conversation, but it's certainly one that can help minimize the fear of unknowns surrounding old age and dying.

It is critical to understand that retirement is not a standardized time in life that simply means life after work, funded by monthly withdrawals from retirement savings accounts with a splash of Social Security on top. It's potentially a multi-decade, multi-phase time in life that requires customized planning that encompasses financial and emotional preparedness. An oversimplified, one-size-fits-all investing blueprint built by large mutual fund companies, banks, and brokerage firms is simply not good enough. You worked too hard for too long to accept that kind of mediocre approach to planning your golden years.

Defining your retirement and properly planning for it is not a small task. It might feel so overwhelming that you decide to let it sit on the back burner to deal with later. Unfortunately, later often becomes too late, and something happens where people are forced to make decisions they are not prepared for.

---

[18] Kimberly Amadeo. The Balance. May 5, 2019. "The Rising Cost of Health Care by Year and Its Causes."
https://www.thebalance.com/causes-of-rising-healthcare-costs-4064878

Let's get retirement off the back burner and take a small step together. Forget Wikipedia and Webster. Let's define your retirement. I'll even give you a head start by letting you see my personal definition of retirement one more time:

> *Retirement: (n) re-tire-mint: a major life transition point where one has achieved financial independence and a clear vision of their life's true purpose. Occupation becomes choice rather than necessity.*

The next step is up to you. Choose wisely how to approach planning, and make sure your financial advisor understands you are a person with complex needs—not just a financial statement that produces monthly retirement income.

Suggestions for Women in Transition—Applies to Men, Too!

A few chapters back, I introduced you to Peter and Tammy; clients of ours who experienced a major life transition after Peter was diagnosed with ALS. Thanks to thoughtful planning, Peter's entire retirement savings remained intact so Tammy would have the opportunity to live worry-free from running out of money during her lifetime. That was the peace of mind they both had, allowing them the freedom to enjoy every minute of their extremely shortened retirement together.

Just shy of five years after experiencing this life changing event of Peter's diagnosis, Tammy was faced with another massive challenge: the death of Peter. Just as a new normal was beginning to set in for Tammy, she was thrust into limbo again and faced with all the uncertainty that came with facing life ahead without Peter. What would Life 3.0 look like? It was nearly impossible to envision for Tammy at first.

Can you relate to the state of limbo Tammy has been forced into again? Have you experienced an unexpected event in life that has thrown you into a state of unknowns? Perhaps you've been recently widowed? Or in the midst of a difficult divorce? Are you a stay-at-home mom ready to re-enter the workforce? Are you a business owner about to take your company public? Have you recently experienced the death of a parent? Are you recently married and considering the start of your family?

If you are a woman (or a man!) and answered yes to any of these questions, you are experiencing a major life transition. It is important to realize that as a woman facing a new life challenge, you now have special financial needs. And you are certainly not alone.

Widowhood is the most common life change we see when we meet a new female client experiencing a major transition. The average American woman lives almost five years longer than the average U.S. man. The Women's Institute for a Secure Retirement also reports half of all widows become so by age sixty-five, and they are more likely than men to lose income after the death of their spouse.[19]

Divorce is the next most common transition that brings a woman to our doorsteps for financial advice. This makes complete sense as the divorce rate in the state of California is now a staggering 50 to 60 percent. More than half of marriages in California end in divorce.[20]

Major life transitions involve strong emotions. Whether these emotions are positive or negative, there is nothing more dangerous to one's financial well-being than combining major money decisions with emotions. You will likely need triage strategies for handling necessary financial decisions during your major transition.

Although your circumstances are unique to you, women in transition face similar challenges.

Most women I meet going through major life changes tell me that feel like they are in limbo, like they are stuck in a thick fog and can't see or think clearly. If you feel this way, you are not alone. Many people get stuck in limbo as a basic coping function to protect themselves from stress and negative emotions.

This state of numbness can also be dangerous when the fog gives us permission to make bad choices with our money or avoid handling the important stuff like paying bills. Whether bills go unpaid, or you start

---

[19] Wiser. "Widowhood Why Women Need to Talk About This Issue." http://www.wiserwomen.org/index.php?id=274

[20] Henry F. Lewis. Gardner & Lewis. October 9, 2018. "Divorce Statistics in the United States and California." https://www.michaelagardner.net/blog/2018/10/09/divorce-statistics-in-the-united-193973

spending impulsively, you can find yourself looking back with an incredible amount of regret. We've met women who have completely depleted their IRAs to travel the world with their best girlfriend to help cope with the loss of their husbands. We have also met women who have not paid their utility bills or mortgages for months and found themselves facing serious credit consequences. Meanwhile, women in transition may also be in a vortex of swirling, conflicting advice from well-meaning, yet often misinformed, friends and family.

Over the many years our firm has helped women in such situations, we have found five basic tips that can help them.

TIP #1: GIVE YOURSELF TIME.

Don't sell your home. Don't re-allocate all your retirement savings. Don't invest your life insurance benefits. Give yourself at least six months to upwards of a year to work through your "fog" before you make any substantial financial decisions. Remember, there is nothing more dangerous to your financial well-being than making big money decisions while emotions are running high. You should seek professional advice on what decisions you can defer and what decisions you cannot defer. When in doubt, take your time.

For help finding professional advice, start by asking a close friend, family member or trusted advisor (e.g. CPA or attorney). If you have no one to rely on for advice, consider visiting www.cfp.net to find a Certified Financial Planner© professional who specializes in helping women in transition. You can also visit our website at www.GebhardtGroupInc.com to learn more about how we help women going through major life changes.

TIP #2: ASK FOR HELP.

Although I recommend you delay large financial decisions, there are everyday decisions that must be made whether you feel up to it or not. Paying your bills is the biggest. If you are struggling to keep up with your daily financial responsibilities, ask for help. Consider asking a close friend or family member to step in and take over this function for you for a while. If you are not comfortable with that, consider hiring a bookkeeper or accountant to handle it for you. Of course, this might incur some cost, but it will be well worth it if it means protecting your credit, keeping you current with your monthly financial obligations, and allowing you necessary emotional and mental space.

Tip #3: Buy Yourself Financial Safety.

Keep your money as liquid as possible, especially if you are experiencing a transition because of the death of a spouse, a divorce, or a significant windfall (sale of a business, loss of a parent, etc.). Liquid assets, such as cash and short-term investments, give you the liquidity net you need in an emotional time of transition. After six months or a year, your needs will change. You will want to preserve as many options as possible and staying liquid and "safe" does just that. However, your money that was invested in the past may or may not suit your needs now.

Tip #4: Try to Stay Healthy.

You will make better choices if you eat right, sleep enough, rest, meditate, and make time for exercise every day. The only person you need to focus on at this point is you. Whether you have children or others that depend on your care, you can only be your best for them if you take care of you first and foremost.

Tip #5: Protect yourself.

Unfortunately, there are devious people in our world who look for an opportunity to take advantage of people in transition, especially women. Many of the women I work with have unintentionally vented their emotional vulnerability during their life change, often through outlets like social media. Be careful of the people offering help. Always have a trusted friend, family member, or advisor as a sounding board before you choose to engage anyone or any business to help you.

Often, devious financial advisors will try to approach a woman in transition to take advantage of her new potential financial windfall. Before you engage a financial advisor that approaches you, visit the Financial Industry Regulatory Agency (FINRA) to perform a background check on him or her.[21]

Hopefully your transition is the result of something great happening in your life, like having your first baby or selling your business. Unfortunately, the women we are introduced to are often experiencing a painful event. Regardless of whether your big life transition is positive or negative, the tips I listed are five important things to consider when it comes to your financial well-being.

I wish you peace and prosperity, and I know with confidence that one day your fog will lift, and you will have the courage to take that necessary step forward in the next great stage of your life.

---

[21] FINRA. BrokerCheck.
https://brokercheck.finra.org

A Threat to Future Financial Security

When I was eighteen years old and headed off to college, we did not have email or smartphones to communicate with friends and family. I used to call my parents collect from a payphone at the end of the hall in my dormitory for 10 cents a minute. I used to write my girlfriend love letters and send them to her in the mail. In 1990, it cost me 25 cents to mail a letter to her. My sophomore year of college, postage rates increased to 29 cents. A year after graduation, the price of a stamp increased to 32 cents.

As of January 2019, the cost of a U.S. postage stamp had increased to 55 cents. Using the rule of 72, we can easily calculate the rate at which the price of a U.S. stamp has increased since my college days—approximately 3 percent a year. That doesn't sound like much, but over time, that annualized price increase can be significant.

The reason I chose to highlight the increase in prices for postage stamps is because they are representative of the long-term average price increase for many of the things we spend our money on: clothing, transportation, most household items, and a lot more. Some years price increases are higher, some years they're lower. But over long periods of time, 3 percent has been the historical norm for lots of things we spend money on. Once more applying the rule of 72, this means that our income and our savings accounts have to double every twenty-four years just to be able to buy us the same stuff in the future that we buy now.

Success or failure in keeping up with the rising cost of stuff is called inflation risk. Inflation risk is something every worker and retirement saver needs to protect themselves against. It means that over time, the cost of "stuff" goes up and our savings and paychecks need to beat or exceed the rate at which "stuff" costs more over long periods of time.

Inflation is measured in a number of ways. The most common form of inflation is measured by what's called the Consumer Price Index (CPI). The CPI measures the growth rate of items consumers spend their money on, minus food and energy cost. It's important to know that CPI is an average that covers many things. Specific things like college education and healthcare see much greater than 3 percent inflation rates year in and year out. Other things like TVs and computers have seen negative inflation, meaning prices have actually decreased over time. But put it all in a blender and we can expect to average 3 percent inflation over our lifetime.

Wall Street and the financial services industry have done a good job educating investors on how inflation can erode one's purchasing power over long periods of time. Many investment tools have been created to help people grow their investment savings in an attempt to outpace inflation.

But there is one side of inflation Wall Street and the financial services industry does not spend enough time addressing and helping people with. It's called **lifestyle inflation**, the official term for 'keeping up with the Joneses.'

Think back to your first full-time job. Do you remember your starting salary?

My first full-time job was as a stockbroker trainee and my initial salary was $22,000. Paying my bills every month wasn't easy. There was barely any money left over to have fun or treat myself to a weekend splurge. I remember thinking often about how much better life would be if I were able to just manage a small pay raise and live more like everyone else I see out there having fun and buying lots of cool stuff.

When I found my next job a year later working for a small mutual fund manufacturer, my salary was increased to $25,000. A $3,000 pay raise was something I was proud of. Naturally I wanted to reward myself for working hard and finding a new job that paid me more. With that pay raise, I found myself eating out more and treating myself to little "extras."

As time went on, I continued to see more significant pay raises. With each pay raise came rewards: a nicer car, a bigger house, fancier suits, more expensive meals; all the necessities for keeping up with everyone around me. By the time I was thirty-three years old, my pay had increased over 2,000 percent from my initial $22,000 salary and my lifestyle had certainly reflected the massive pay increase over time. I felt like I was now Mr. Jones himself!

My income had outpaced inflation by a long shot—only now my financial obligations had become much greater and way more complex, thanks to my desire to keep up. I owned a much bigger home, which meant higher utility and maintenance. Of course, we had to hire a gardener and house cleaners, since everyone else in the neighborhood did this, too. Since the new home was bigger, it seemed appropriate to buy more furniture and decorations to fill the empty space. My new European sports sedans also came with higher costs of ownership: high-test gasoline and maintenance costs like synthetic oil changes and high-end brake replacements.

Despite seeing my income grow much faster than 3 percent inflation, I ultimately found myself in the same exact place I was when I was twenty-two years old with a $22,000 salary: able to pay my bills but with little in savings to show for all my efforts. Despite having much nicer stuff, the respect of the Joneses, and a whole bunch more financial complexity in my life, the one thing I did not have more of was money in the bank or significantly more in retirement savings.

Lifestyle inflation is the single greatest risk to one's financial security in retirement. It's much more dangerous than the risk of core inflation. But the good news is that, unlike core inflation risk, lifestyle inflation is something we have 100 percent control over.

Most new clients I meet tell me they have experienced lifestyle inflation. I often meet people who make lots of money and they tell me they have no idea where it goes every month. The list of financial obligations they bring in for review is daunting. House payments, private school tuition, country club memberships, Neiman Marcus charge cards, multiple lease payments for cars and boats—they often feel overwhelmed, stuck, and unable to see how to unwind this high rate of lifestyle inflation that's now suffocating them.

I start by reminding them they're not alone, that I've been where they are, as have so many others. But now, unlike most people, who never learn about lifestyle inflation until it's too late, we get to change behaviors, unwind the complexity that's been created, and start to reverse the damaging effects lifestyle inflation will continue to have on their future financial security in retirement.

If the best time to plant a tree was twenty years ago, the next best time is now.

What I mean by that is, once we become aware of the damaging effects of lifestyle inflation, we can choose to make smarter choices starting right now.

Pay raises going forward can be directed into savings instead of spending. Instead of using the next pay raise to keep up with the Joneses with vacations, nicer cars, and home improvements, the increased net amount received in your paycheck could be automatically swept into one form of savings for the future. If your emergency savings is less than six months' worth of living expenses, then I recommend we start there. Once six months' worth of living expenses are set aside, then we can start using the pay increase to add extra funding to your financial vehicles of choice, like a 401(k), IRA, Roth IRA, or cash-value life insurance policy.

I am all for enjoying a nice vacation or paying for some upkeep on a home. But these are items that can be funded with some planning and disciplined savings strategies rather than just being absorbed by annual pay increases. Perhaps a portion of your pay raise can go toward discretionary spending. But I have learned firsthand that real financial security often comes from having six to twelve months of income saved, and enough retirement savings accumulated to create thirty or more years of retirement income. It does not come from having lots of nice stuff.

Lifestyle inflation comes mostly from our need to keep up with the Joneses. Most of us succumb to it at some point in our lives. Our neighbor buys a new car, then so must we. A friend posts pictures on social media of a lavish Hawaiian vacation and so we book a similar trip for our family. *Comparison is the foundation of all unhappiness* and our desire to keep up with the Joneses ultimately becomes our financial downfall when we reach retirement age.

Inflation risk is real. But the price at which things we purchase increases is completely out of our control. Lifestyle inflation, which has a much greater effect on our financial security in retirement, is the one aspect of inflation risk we have complete control over.

Forget the Joneses. Take care of yourself and your family. I promise one day you'll be grateful you did.

Common Myths That Hurt Retirement Savers

An old friend and I were having lunch. He seemed frustrated when we sat down at our table. Before we even opened our menus, I asked him if there was something on his mind.

Without hesitation, he began sharing how his financial advisor had failed to keep up with the market, with the result that his retirement savings was significantly underperforming. He was adamant about firing his advisor and hiring my firm to take over the day-to-day management of his portfolio.

After asking a few more questions and listening carefully, I was able to help my friend see that his portfolio was doing exactly what it needed to be doing for his retirement. I politely declined his offer. I knew my friend's advisor. This individual cares deeply for her clients, provides excellent service, and is extremely good at what she does.

My friend had unfortunately bought into one of three common myths that can really hurt retirement savers: believing that you must beat the market.

More about that in a minute.

Even with good guidance from a professional wealth advisor, navigating Wall Street and the retirement savings sphere can be scary, unclear, and awash in myths for the average investor. With a twenty-four-hour news cycle on television and instantaneous access to current market events on their smartphones, everyday retirement savers are often lured into believing what the media machine wants them to believe. I saw this firsthand having lunch with my old friend, and I see it every day in my conversations with others. Becoming aware of these mythological beliefs is a crucial first step for retirement savers to successfully traverse their way to a secure retirement.

Myth #1: You must beat the market.

One of the first discussions I have with prospective clients is a deep dive into the most important long-term goals they have for themselves and their families. Over the past twenty years of having these discussions, I have yet to hear someone tell me their top goal is to beat the market or a market index.

People describe their ideal future and seek help reaching financial thresholds that allow them to do what they enjoy most with who they love most. These important goals have nothing to do with beating an index. Reaching these goals is rarely, if ever, dependent upon beating a market index.

It's easy to understand where the myth that you must beat the market came from. As pensions started disappearing *en masse* in the 1980s and 1990s, more and more people began investing through vehicles like retirement plans and IRA accounts. This influx of new investment capital drove markets to all-time heights. In the 1990s, investors saw returns that doubled their money every two or three years. As a result, people flocked to the market as the 1990s ended, with hopes of creating enormous wealth. This led many to the belief that the success of their portfolio depended on beating the market.

The S&P 500 Index has a long-term average of about 10 percent per year since 1926 according to an article published on the website NerdWallet.[22] Wall Street brokerage firm mythology has many believing that this represents the entire market; that it's the bull's eye. According to the mythology, it's the primary responsibility of the advisor or portfolio manager to outperform this index each and every year based on what happened in the 1990s.

---

[22] James Royal & Arielle O'Shea. Nerdwallet. May 15, 2019. "What Is the Average Stock Market Return?"
https://www.nerdwallet.com/blog/investing/average-stock-market-return/

The reality is the S&P 500 only represents a fraction of the broad market, made up of the largest 500 companies in America. That's a small slice of the worldwide market, and it's a return that requires taking on substantial risk with one's retirement savings to beat.

The whole concept of risk relative to market returns is misunderstood. Many people we meet are willing to take more risk in good markets and less risk in bad markets . . . except it doesn't really work that way!

I believe your long-term wealth is something you will acquire through *your occupation and your discipline to save money.* Your investment portfolio is a place for you to protect that wealth and help ensure it maintains its purchasing power (beats inflation) over time. With long-term inflation at 2 to 3 percent, I believe that most retirement savers have the ability to reach their most important goals with far less return (and far less risk) than that of the S&P 500.

Your portfolio is likely the largest part of your savings and should not be thrown completely to the stock market roller coaster. It should be viewed as an investment vehicle designed to create *security, stability, and predictability for your most important life objectives.* Trying to beat the market requires a gambler's mentality, which could be extremely dangerous for one's financial well-being. Having a small portion of your overall portfolio allocated to "play money" or gambling money that takes substantial risks is fine. However, I usually recommend this never be more than 5 percent of your total portfolio, depending on your unique circumstances. In fact, you might just be better off taking that money to Las Vegas, rather than gambling with it in high risk stuff in the market. At least in Vegas you can gamble and be entertained at the same time!

MYTH #2: "BUY AND HOLD" INVESTING IS THE BEST APPROACH.

One of the most common myths propagated by Wall Street brokerage firms and mainstream media is the belief that you can simply put your portfolio on autopilot, staying passively invested while you ride the market waves up and down hoping it works out for you one day when you need it. The sales pitch supporting the myth of passive investing is convincing: missing out on the ten to twenty best days of the market each year can cost most of your return.

But the devil is in the details. What would happen if you also missed the ten to twenty worst-performing days of the market each year? Your return actually *increases!* The buy-and-hold sales pitch leaves that part out. It also leaves out the reality that passive investing has failed millions of retirement savers twice already in the twenty-first century: once during the dot-com bubble of 2000 to 2002, and again during the Great Recession of 2008 to 2009. In both of those bear markets, passive buy-and-hold investors lost anywhere between 25 and 60 percent of their retirement savings. Some investors who stayed invested post-recession in 2008 were able to recover most of their losses in about six years. For those who stayed invested through the dot-com bubble to 2000, it took just over eight years.[23] But for those standing on the doorsteps of retirement right before either of those two epic market drops, imagine seeing your million-dollar retirement lose $250,000 to $600,000 right before you needed it to replace your working income. What would that do to your plans regarding the first few years of retirement?

Proper portfolio management requires a dynamic approach that matches the busy, dynamic lives real people live. As goals and market environments change, so must one's portfolio. A portfolio requires ongoing maintenance, monitoring, and reallocating as trends in markets shift over one's lifetime. Betting solely on a passive allocation, "setting it and forgetting it," is a disaster waiting to happen come the next bear market.

Remember, Wall Street brokers and the big fund companies only earn their fees if you remain fully invested, passively riding the market waves up and down. The minute you adjust your portfolio to reflect a

---

[23] Zach. Four Pillar Freedom. June 21, 2008. "Here's How Long the Stock Market Has Historically Taken to Recover from Drops." https://fourpillarfreedom.com/heres-how-long-the-stock-market-has-historically-taken-to-recover-from-drops/

more defensive position (moving money to cash) is when brokers and the big fund companies lose. And they don't like to lose.

MYTH #3: YOUR BROKER HAS YOUR BACK.

A dear friend of mine lost her husband several years back. She told me how the best man in their wedding stepped in to help her right after her husband died. He was a lifelong trusted friend and called himself a "financial advisor." He assured her he would put her money in something safe, something "guaranteed not to lose money." His words, not mine.

At the time, that sounded good to my friend. But two years later when she needed $28,000 to replace the roof on her house, she found she would be assessed a large surrender penalty for taking money out of that "safe" product her friend had sold her.

The product was an equity-indexed annuity. There is absolutely nothing wrong with an equity-indexed annuity if it's used in the right circumstances. But in my friend's case, she already had plenty of income from her rental properties, and her liquid assets were already tax-deferred because they were held in an IRA. There didn't appear to be any real benefit to her to owning this annuity product whatsoever.

Then we figured out how much commission the advisor made by selling her this product: $40,000! He earned an 8 percent upfront commission by selling my dear friend an investment that was not in her best interest. And she hasn't heard from him since.

There are plenty of honest, ethical advisors in financial services. But there are also many who are not. Even within the sphere of "honest and ethical," there exists a fine line that can create a lot of conflict of interest when advising clients on what to do with their money. Simply put, any advisor who earns a commission paid by a mutual fund company, a brokerage firm, or an insurance company is opening the door for conflict of interest. And often it is the financial interest of the advisor that (legally) wins out.

Commission-based advisors are brokers. They are salespeople. They are licensed by the Financial Industry Regulatory Authority

(FINRA) to sell securities for a commission and are required by law to apply the "suitability standard" to a securities sale. That means that they must make sure an investment is suitable based on the client's age, investment experience, risk tolerance, and a handful of other factors before they can sell it to a client and earn a commission. But if that investment also happens to be the most expensive in its category because it pays a higher commission to the broker than some lower-cost equivalents, that broker can legally make that sale, even if it's not in the best interest of his client.

I rarely earn commissions for selling investment products. Only when it is in my clients' best interest and there is no other option do we provide them with products that pay commissions from an insurance company. In some circumstances, we do not have a choice. For example, certain types of annuities that provide lifetime income can be in the best interest of some clients for a portion of their retirement savings. Often, we meet people who are significantly underinsured when it comes to life insurance. Therefore, we will generally recommend the least-expensive term policy we can find to fill their insurance gap. These products do pay us a modest commission. However, in situations like these, we uphold our obligation to serve the best interest of our clients and find the best products in the annuity and insurance world with no bias to any one insurer, regardless of the compensation to our firm.

With rare exceptions, most of our revenue comes from advisory fees we charge our clients directly. In most cases, the only one paying us is our client. We are completely investment-agnostic, and generally recommend low-cost, index-based ETFs to our clients. It is our belief that investments are commodities, and the expenses associated with owning these commodities should be kept as low as possible. By charging fees directly to our clients, we are also obligated by federal law to uphold the *fiduciary standard*, meaning we must put our clients' best interest ahead of our own and eliminate all conflict of interest. By taking a fiduciary role in the lives of our clients, they know we have their backs.

Bottom line: To assure yourself that your advisor has your best interest in mind, I suggest you pick one who is primarily fee-based when it comes to the investable assets you entrust them to manage. If an advisor uses some commission-based products to run their business, that's probably fine, as long as he or she does not rely exclusively on these to earn a living. Salespeople who are 100 percent commission-based are fine for purchasing cars or furniture, but they may not be the best option for helping you achieve your most important financial goals.

Finding a trusted advisor is an important rest stop on the road to building true wealth. Whether you are just graduating school and wondering how to buy a few stocks, or you're a seasoned investor ready to transition from building your wealth to protecting it, there are great advisors out there for you. Most people I meet have an incredible sense about others. Trust yourself; you'll know when you've found someone you can rely on to have your back with your wealth.

One of my early mentors used to have a funny spin on an old saying you might be familiar with: "If it's too good to be true, it may not be. But if it's too good to be true, it's definitely too good to be free!"

Challenging the Status Quo
A NEW APPROACH TO PROTECTING AND GROWING MONEY
THAT IS COMPLETELY COUNTER TO THE CULTURE

For decades, Wall Street brokerage firms have promoted investment strategies based on hunches and intuitions. Their predictive-based strategies eventually evolved to using more academic-based theories (statistics and formulas) to try to predict better what "ought to" happen in the markets and how investors "ought to" behave as a result. Not only were these predictive-based and theory-based approaches to investing subjective, they were often inconsistent.

I believe this approach is unsound and outdated, and no longer serves the complex needs of investors in the 21st century. In this chapter, I will introduce you to a modern approach to saving, investing, and protecting your assets that goes one step further than the basics I have outlined thus far.

To illustrate, let's look at a story from Major League Baseball.

When Paul DiPodesta walked into the office of Oakland A's general manager Billy Beane, the game of baseball changed forever. It was 1999, and the A's were a small-budget team suffering a drought of post-season appearances. The collaboration of DiPodesta and Beane produced a transformation in how teams would manage for success moving forward. Their baby was a new statistical approach to player trend analysis called Sabermetrics—a transition in baseball history that was perfectly reflected in Michael Lewis' book *Moneyball*.

Prior to the pairing of these two young, unlikely characters, front offices across the major leagues were filled with stodgy game veterans. General managers were usually former players who had been around the game for decades, sitting in their plush offices, smoking cigars, trying to figure out how they could keep their franchise superstars happy and productive. They made staffing decisions based on hunches and intuition, and money was king. The GMs with the biggest payrolls saw the most playoff opportunities for their teams. They rode their franchise players up and down the waves of a normal baseball career through streaks and slumps, hoping that streaks would last forever and slumps would end quickly. Players didn't move around much. They stayed with one or two teams for the majority of their careers and retired with the hopes of managing in the dugout or the front office one day.

Before 1999, GMs used some statistics to support their hunches and intuitive tendencies. But these numbers were subjective and often flawed, in the eyes of Beane and DiPodesta. Statistics such as stolen bases, runs batted in, and batting average, typically used to gauge players, produced an outdated view of the game relative to the statistics available at that time. Billy Beane and Paul DiPodesta began taking advantage of more analytical gauges of player performance to field a team that could better compete against the biggest payrolls in Major League Baseball.

Beane and DiPodesta began studying modern statistical analysis and player trends at great lengths. Their research found on-base and slugging percentages were better indicators of a team's ability to score runs and obtain offensive success. Beane was also convinced these attributes were cheaper to secure on the open market than more historically valued measures such as power, speed, and contact. His convictions caused great controversy between Beane and his scouts, who favored sticking with more traditional baseball wisdom of hunches and intuition. But Beane was hell-bent on flying in the face of the old ways; he was obsessed with going counter to the culture.

Despite a few years of constant battling, Beane eventually gained the support of his players, team owner and staff. By challenging the status quo of old-world baseball beliefs and radically changing the strategies that produce wins on the field, the 2002 Athletics and Billy

Beane, with a $44 million payroll, were able to compete with the $125 million payroll of the mighty New York Yankees. This new approach to playing "moneyball" brought the A's to the playoffs in 2002 and 2003. They have remained one of the most consistently competitive teams in baseball ever since.

By the beginning of 2004, teams across the sport were adjusting their approach to selecting their rosters, mirroring the trend started by Billy Beane and Paul DiPodesta in 1999. Sabermetrics had taken hold of baseball and transformed the game as we know it today.

Thanks to new technologies and modern thinking that challenged the status quo, the front office leaders of baseball went from riding franchise players up and down the cycles of streaks and slumps, hoping for a shot at the playoffs, to applying trend analysis and statistical evaluation for determining their best chances at victory.

I use this story to illustrate some direct parallels that we, as investors and retirement savers, need to consider. As I mentioned earlier, Wall Street brokerage firms have traditionally pushed investment strategies based on hunches and intuition—just like old-time baseball managers—and I believe they're off-base. The proof of their flaws came to light in the first ten years of the 21st century. These predictive and theory-based investment strategies created what's been called "the lost decade" for everyday investors and retirement savers. In fact, millions of people lost 20, 30, even 40 percent of their life savings in 2008 and 2009 by quietly following the obsolete advice of big Wall Street brokerage firms.

Like Sabermetrics in baseball, there is a fact-based approach to analyzing trends and statistics in global markets that is available to investors like you and me. It will require you to begin questioning if there may, in fact, be a better way to manage your investments than what you currently are doing. Is there a strategy different from simply riding the market waves up and down, *hoping* for a shot at the playoffs?

In case you were wondering, there is.

Here's a little cap to the Billy Beane story. In 2003, John Henry, owner of the Boston Red Sox, became such a believer in Sabermetrics that he offered Billy Beane the largest paycheck ever for a baseball GM. Beane graciously turned it down so he could stay in Oakland. Of course, the Boston Red Sox went on to win the World Series the following season. By applying this new approach to trend analysis, Mr. Henry and his Red Sox were able to defeat the curse that had haunted them for decades.

Why was Mr. Henry such a believer? He recognized Sabermetrics as a trend-based approach similar to what he relied on for building and protecting his billion-dollar fortune in the commodities market. That strategy was called *mechanical trend following*, and it proved so successful that Mr. Henry used it to establish John W. Henry & Company, Inc. in 1981. His firm's approach to managing commodities for retail clients was based on automated trading decisions that were in response to trend reversals in each market's direction. Mr. Henry's primary goal was to *eliminate human emotion*, as well as subjective evaluation of such things as the so-called economic fundamentals that traditionally had been relied on by most commodities traders.

Henry's approach was almost identical to the one my firm subscribes to, though we apply trend analysis to the stock market rather than the commodities market. We call it *fact-based investing*, and it applies quantitative trend analysis as the engine driving investment decisions. Fact-based investing is completely counter to the culture of Wall Street brokerage firms. Like Sabermetrics in baseball, it will ultimately transform the way people view and invest their hard-earned assets in the world of the stock market.

Bringing It All Together
CAN OLD DOGS LEARN NEW TRICKS?

A good friend of mine recently asked for my advice about what to do with his life savings. It had become substantial and he was worried about losing it. He said, "Matthew, I understand that your life's work is about challenging the status quo, that you've developed a unique belief system about managing your money and defining true wealth through three key relationships. Being able to quickly transition from offense to defense with my money seems smart, but everyone has always told me that buy-and-hold investing is the way to go. It's all I know, and it's what I'm comfortable with. Maybe you really can't teach old dogs new tricks."

"You can't teach an old dog new tricks" is one of the oldest idioms in the English language. I would bet big money that, over my twenty-year career in financial services, I've heard that saying at least a thousand times.

Well, I don't buy it. For one thing, old dogs can absolutely learn "new tricks." Life is constantly evolving, and technology is improving exponentially, from communications to online banking and strategies for managing your retirement.

When my son, Miles, was two years old, we took him to see his first movie in the theater: *Monsters, Inc.* Miles was instantly in love with it. *Monsters, Inc.* became his life. Mike and Sully, the two main characters, were his new best friends. Over the next few months, our house was littered with every *Monsters, Inc.* piece of paraphernalia ever created.

About a year later, we took Miles to *Finding Nemo*. As a *Monsters, Inc.* loyalist, he had absolutely no interest in a movie about fish. As

Miles lay on the floor of the theater lobby in full tantrum mode, refusing to see a movie about anything but monsters, I was this close to losing my you-know-what. I carried him kicking and screaming into the theater. But, as it happened, we walked in about a minute into the film, during the scene where Nemo's mom is chomped by a barracuda. This would normally be a scary thing for a three-year old, but not my kid who loved monsters!

Miles was instantly hooked. Much like his first experience with *Monsters, Inc.*, he fell completely in love with *Finding Nemo*.

I could repeat this story for the next several Pixar films. It took until my son was seven or eight before he realized he might actually like the next film. He was so stuck in his ways, refusing to accept the possibility of any other option.

The reason I tell this story goes back to the idea that you can't teach an old dog new tricks. As I've already said, people learn new tricks all the time. And learning them is something we resist from a young age. As my son's story proves, we do not wait until we're old to resist learning something outside our comfort zone. But with enough encouragement and coaching, anyone can learn to adapt to something new, even my stubborn three-year-old.

For some people, like my good friend who sought my investment advice, it's challenging to break away from obsolete buy-and-hold (buy-and-hope!) investment advice. It's easy to stay with the familiar. But mixing feelings and emotions with your retirement funding decisions is a dangerous business. Nothing can lead to bad financial decisions more than allowing emotion to creep into the process.

Buy-hold-hope investing worked during the longest bull market in history, from 1984 to 1999. But that market was preceded and followed by decades of stagnant returns, costing investors billions of dollars in lost retirement savings.

I'm coming across more and more people today who are pretty sure that hope is not the strategy they want to bet their retirement on. They're motivated to break away from traditional Wall Street thinking. They realize the reality that retirement is on their shoulders and they can't risk blowing it by relying on hope.

Are you sick and tired of riding the market waves up and down hoping it all works out for you one day? Have you ever looked at your portfolio or retirement statements and wondered if there was a better way to manage it all?

If you answered "yes" to either question, it's time for you to consider another option.

You can gain control of your retirement savings. You can retire on your terms. And there absolutely is a better way to manage it all. More on that should we get to meet one another in person, I promise. But first, let's look at a couple more stories as evidence of forward-thinking leadership and learning new ways of doing business.

XEROX AND KODAK

About six hours northwest of New York City is Rochester, infamously known for its bitter cold winters. Rochester is also known for being the home of two deeply rooted names in corporate American history: Xerox and Kodak.

Both companies have struggled greatly as 21st-century America has embraced the digital age. Kodak was once synonymous with photography. Despite holding many patents, the company is now for sale to the highest bidder as a result of its failure to modernize and embrace the digital movement. The bottom line for Kodak is that the old dog refused to learn new tricks.

The same could also be said about Xerox, which started digging in its corporate heels during the late 1990s. They were going to remain a document company no matter what—another old dog refusing (at first) to learn new tricks. Although Xerox made some smart acquisitions and the company is now back on track to provide steady growth, it had a shaky transition into the 21st century.

What is the lesson to learn from Kodak and Xerox? Both were mega-corporations, accounting for tens of thousands of jobs and providing prosperity for much of Greater Rochester. A culture of leadership that refused to adapt as markets and customers' needs changed ultimately cost that great community much of the opulence those companies once created.

Thankfully, not all old corporations think like old dogs that refuse to learn a new trick or two. In 2015, Google, Intel, and luxury watchmaker TAG Heuer created a partnership to launch an Android-based smartwatch, promising an elegant alternative to the Apple Watch. Jean-Claude Biver, CEO of TAG Heuer, called the partnership "a marriage of technological innovation with watchmaking credibility."[24] What excited me most about this announcement is that TAG Heuer is a Swiss watchmaker that has been in business since 1860! Talk about an old dog learning a new trick. When a company that's been in business for more than 150 years teams up with some of the most modern and youthful technology organizations to combine classic and elegant with modern and cutting-edge, that's very cool, and it clearly demonstrates forward-thinking leadership.

There is a similar lesson to be learned in the space of planning a secure retirement. Old dogs who refuse to accept that the face of retirement planning has radically changed will wake up one day looking like Kodak, which is now a nearly defunct organization. Today, pensions have all but disappeared, forcing people to do their own heavy lifting when it comes to the financial piece of retirement.

The big mutual fund companies attempted to "assist" by jumping into the retirement business in the 1980s. There were huge profits to be made by fund companies for entering this market, especially if retirement savers automatically added money every month and kept it all fully invested. The fees charged and earned by the big fund companies became enormous, and their marketing tactics kept the majority of retirement savers sitting still, quietly riding the market waves up and down.

---

[24] BusinessWire. March 19, 2019. "TAG Heuer, Google and Intel Announce Swiss Smarthwatch Collaboration." https://www.businesswire.com/news/home/20150319005152/en/TAG-Heuer-Google-Intel-Announce-Swiss-Smartwatch

The entrance of the 21st century created the catalyst for change when it came to planning for a secure retirement. The "lost decade" of 2000 to 2009 proved that 20th-century mainstream advice—simple asset allocation, diversification, buy-and-hold investing—didn't always work for an aging baby boomer population of nearly 78 million investors. In particular, retirement savers were left with gaping losses, and many who planned to retire could not retire the way they initially planned to retire. [25]

The good news is retirement savers no longer must rely on old-dog advice from old-dog Wall Street brokerage firms and mutual fund companies. This is one of the biggest reasons why my partner and I created Gebhardt Group, Inc. We wanted to give investors the ongoing, personalized advice they deserve to protect their most important financial assets. Unlike some of the big Wall Street brokerage firms, we get you. We *are* you.

As I said earlier in this chapter, I've been told countless times over my twenty-year career that you cannot teach old dogs new tricks. I don't buy it, because the only constant in this world is change. Everyone is capable of learning something new, adapting, and being prepared for what comes next. Fortunately for Rochester, Xerox has finally figured that out. A 155-year old watch-maker has also figured it out.

Have you? If you're still riding the market up and down with your investment savings, hoping it all works out one day, think again. What happens to your retirement if Wall Street is wrong? What happens to all the plans you've made and the dreams you've dreamt if the next big bear market happens the year before you plan to retire? What would the consequences be for you, your family, your health, your legacy?

---

[25] Teresa Ghilarducci. The Atlantic. October 16, 2015. "The Recession Hurt Americans' Retirement Accounts More Than Anybody Knew." https://www.theatlantic.com/business/archive/2015/10/the-recession-hurt-americans-retirement-accounts-more-than-everyone-thought/410791/

Some Final Thoughts

You have the capacity to learn new tricks when it comes to how you measure and value your true wealth. I always thought if I could make and save lots of money, I would be able to take care of the people who mattered most to me. If I were able to do that, then I would be able to look in the mirror and feel good about myself. But something early in life triggered me to begin chasing comfort and pleasure. I got addicted to it. The more I chased money and gave in to what society taught me to value, the more pain and suffering I experienced.

I believe that our society is overrun by a Keeping Up with the Joneses mentality. It's suffocating our relationships with the people we love most. It's destroying our ability to find real financial security in our lives. It's leaving us feeling empty inside. The number one driver of economic growth today is spending. The more times we swipe our credit cards, the better off America is, economically speaking. This is insanity at its best. The economic drive means government, big business, academia, and the media are all incentivized to push us to behaviors that are completely counter to our personal wellbeing. Consumerism: buying the next coolest gadget, going on over-the-top vacations, driving new cars, and buying homes that are way above our means is where society wants us.

Thankfully, you've made an intentional decision to shut yourself off from the noise that's eating away at your soul. You've made a choice to begin seeing what true wealth is about. You've learned to say no more and say yes to the people, places and experiences that bring real joy into your life. You have chosen to live a truly wealthy life. Thank you for your bravery to challenge the status quo with me, to become part of a growing community of like-hearted feelers, who no longer subscribe to the conventional thinking of the everyday, average American. I am honored to be by your side.

If, after reading this book, you feel like you want more, please reach out to me. Rebuilding your wealth one relationship at a time requires daily work, discipline, and a lot of persistence. Reading this book is just a start. I would be honored to continue your journey with you on a much more personal, meaningful level.

I was born to challenge the status quo and inspire others to do the same. If you feel like you're ready, then let's move forward together and plug into our growing community of like-hearted people who are learning to love the person looking at them in the mirror, surrounding themselves with people who bring great joy into their lives, and live with a level of financial security few people truly have.

About the Author

Matthew David Grishman is an author, speaker, coach, and co-owner of Gebhardt Group, Inc.

Coaching is Matthew's passion. He is obsessed with challenging the status quo. Matthew has unique beliefs about money and true wealth that are completely counter to the Wall Street culture he was raised in. His unique ability is to inspire others to reach beyond their limits to live a full, authentic, meaningful life. Whether Matthew is helping a family connect their money to their core personal values, guiding other wealth advisors to do the same work, or coaching the youth in his community about life through the great games of baseball and basketball, Matthew shows up and gives it his all each and every day.

Matthew began his career in financial services in 1995 with A.G. Edwards & Sons, Inc., and became fully licensed as an Investment Broker in 1996. He spent seventeen years as a national spokesperson for large mutual fund and insurance companies (Lord, Abbett & Co; Putnam; and MetLife).

Matthew left corporate America in 2011 to devote his time and experience in financial services to his family, friends, and neighbors. In 2014, Matthew joined Gebhardt Group, Inc., as an independent Registered Investment Advisor. He became an owner of the firm in 2015. As a Principal and Wealth Advisor of Gebhardt Group, Inc., Matthew provides wealth management services for families experiencing major life transitions (inheritance, sale of a business, death or divorce of a spouse, planning for retirement, career change, or sudden loss of a job).

Matthew resides with his wife, Amie, and their two sons, Miles and Lucas, in Rocklin, California. When not working with clients, Matthew spends his time tending the fruit trees in his backyard and exploring amazing places with his family, like Yosemite National Park, the California coast, and big cities around the world.

Matthew and his family have become boots-on-the-ground volunteers for NECHAMA, a worldwide relief organization that provides clean up and recovery assistance to homes and businesses affected by disaster. Matthew is also a member of the Rocklin and Roseville Chambers of Commerce and is active in their leadership training programs for local business owners.

Matthew received a Bachelor of Arts degree in Political Science and Sociology from the State University of New York at Albany in Albany, New York, in June of 1994. He holds a State of California Insurance License #0D99998 for Life, Accident, Disability, and Health Insurance. His securities registrations include the Series 65.

Made in United States
Troutdale, OR
01/06/2024